Sally Randall

free
INDEED

THE**UPWARD***press*

WITH THANKS & DEDICATION...

To all who have encouraged us along the way, you may never know how much your love and support lifted us when the going was tough. We are so thankful for every prayer and for every gentle and not so gentle nudge to put this all together into the book you now hold. It has been a long and sometimes very difficult journey as we have lived out all we have written. We are deeply humbled and grateful for all who believed in us and in the message the Lord has chosen to speak through us.

We thank and honor our parents, our beloved husbands Greg Randall and Steve Jacks, and our entire families for being supportive, encouraging, and prayerful. We love you dearly!

Thank you to Jessica Jacks and Ashley Olson, our wonderful editors. Special thanks to Kathy Olson and Jessica Jacks, whose input onto these pages is immeasurable! Your wisdom and discernment helped guide what is written as you lived out these truths along with us. We treasure and honor you both!

We dedicate this work to the glory of God. We pray that it will bless you and cause you to grow in ways you never knew possible. May His Presence draw you into receiving more of His love, grace, mercy, and freedom—to the glory of God alone!

TABLE OF CONTENTS

free INDEED

IDENTIFY the issue:
John 8:31-32
Philippians 1:9-11
Ephesians 1:17
Luke 11:9-10

NEED Jesus:
John 14:6
Romans 3:23
1 John 1:9
Hebrews 12:10-11
Revelation 12:11
Titus 3:4-7

DISAGREE with the lie or ungodly belief:
John 8:44
Revelation 8:1-2
Romans 8:1-2
Titus 3:3

EVICT the enemy:
Mathew 10:8
Mathew 16:19
Romans 10:9
1 John 4:4

EXALT the LORD:
Jude 1:24-25
Romans 4:20b
Daniel 4:37
Psalm 99:5

DECLARE the truth:
Romans 6:22
Romans 8:37-39
Galatians 5:1
2 Peter 1:3

INTRODUCTION

For all who are led by the Spirit of God are sons of God. For you did not receive a spirit of slavery that returns you to fear, but you received the Spirit of sonship, by whom we cry, "Abba! Father!" The Spirit Himself testifies with our spirit that we are God's children (Romans 8:14-16).[1]

So if the Son sets you free, you will be free indeed (John 8:36).

If you continue in My word, you are truly My disciples. Then you will know the truth, and the truth will set you free (John 8:31b-32).

This project began as a small Bible study with a handful of folks experiencing homelessness. It grew into a series of teachings presented in residential treatment facilities, churches, and small group settings. We began to write what we were learning and teaching because we wanted to help others (and ourselves) live more fully in the freedom for which Christ has set us free. For various reasons, Christians struggle to walk in freedom. Our issues vary from addiction to worry to depression or loneliness, helplessness, anxiety, frustration, procrastination, anger, self-pity, isolation, pride, apathy, stubbornness, passivity, fear, shame, jealousy, rejection, and so on. Whatever the specifics, our struggle against deception and temptation is common to us all (1 Corinthians 10:13).

What is freedom in Christ?

The struggle is so real, in fact, that we may even question if it's possible to experience freedom in Christ this side of heaven. Can we really experience the intimate love of Christ without shame or fear of punishment? Can we really be "free indeed"? What even is freedom, and what does it look like?

First, freedom in Christ is multi-faceted because we are triune beings fashioned after a triune God. "The redemption that is in Jesus is total, involving every aspect of the person," including body, soul (mind, will, emotions), and spirit.[2] Sometimes, we primarily need physical healing. Other times, we need to focus on mental and emotional healing. Sometimes, our freedom depends upon receiving spiritual deliverance from demonic torment. More often than not, a disciplined pursuit of greater freedom in Christ will mean all of the above.

---

1 Unless otherwise noted, all scripture quotations are from the *Berean Study Bible*.
2 Foster, R. J. (1992). *Prayer: Finding the heart's true home*. Harper Collins, p. 203.

Second, freedom in Christ is dynamic and growth oriented. No matter who you are or how long you've been a Christian, you can INDEED grow in the freedom that is found in ever-increasing intimacy with Jesus, free of reproach. Free of the need to perform. Free of fear. His love is limitless, and His grace knows no bounds. There is always more in God than we have yet to understand (Romans 11:33). Freedom and joy are not a destination we reach or a trophy we display, but rather are found in the journey we take with Jesus.

Finally, it is common to think of freedom as the absence of restraint—the ability to do anything we feel like doing whenever we feel like doing it. But absolute freedom in this sense is not what we're talking about. As Richard Foster observes, "Absolute freedom is absolute nonsense! We gain freedom in anything through commitment, discipline, and fixed habit."[3] So how do we get commitment and discipline? Well, to begin with, we begin. We make an effort. We do something that moves us toward rather than away from the God who loves us. Deciding to read this book is something. Following through with the practical applications is something. Picking the book up again and trying the applications again after some time has passed is something. Commitment is built through continued effort. We keep choosing to move toward God. It may help to think about freedom as a journey similar to a fitness journey. Commitment and discipline lead to freedom just as they lead to fitness. Routine, repetition, and rest get results! It also helps to track your progress and to have a personal trainer who can guide you along the way.

Is this for me?

We have written for those who have been walking with Christ for some time but may feel stuck. And for those who may be struggling in a particular area, unable to get free on their own. For those who are hungry for more in their life with Christ. We write for those who might be discouraged, frustrated, or unsure whether freedom is even possible. We, too, have had times when we doubted the possibility of experiencing true freedom this side of heaven. Negative life experiences can powerfully contradict the gospel of freedom, shouting lies designed to paralyze our progress and shipwreck our faith. But freedom is not only possible, it is our inheritance as God's children. We have prayed that God would put this book into the hands of those who need it. We pray for hope to arise off the pages as you read it and for the Holy Spirit to speak His love and healing over you.

---

3 Foster, *Prayer*, 67.

How should I use this book?

We know that the truths we share have literally saved
process of writing and editing has resulted in even dee
and growth. We do not offer untested ideas or merely t
we've lived this stuff—the good, the bad, and the unc
applied these principles and done the work, and as a r
and deepened. At times our freedom has come in sudden, amazing moments
of revelation—the Spirit of God pouring love and truth into our hearts
(Romans 5:5). We have been delivered from tormenting spirits sent by the
enemy to afflict and harass. At other times, we have only recognized growth
and freedom after a slower, subtler process. Whatever the pace, change
begins when we want freedom more than comfort, control, independence,
or anything else that isn't of God.

What we're trying to say is that this book is not meant to be just another
"Christian Living" book that you read and forget. The truths we explain, the
practices we recommend, and the exercises we suggest are meant to be
applied and implemented in your own life and context. We know that if you
actively engage your mind and heart with this material and do the practical
applications, then you will begin to experience increasing freedom in spirit,
soul, and body. We have seen it happen in our own lives and in the lives
of others! We pray it happens for you, too. And we pray that you find a friend
who is willing to walk the journey with you. Indeed, *two are better than
one, because they have a good return for their labor. For if one falls down, his
companion can lift him up; but pity the one who falls without another to help him
up* (Ecclesiastes 4:9-10).

Is this stuff Biblical?

We have done our best to ensure that what we present aligns with sound
doctrine and Biblical truth. If there are doctrinal or Biblical errors in these
pages, they reflect on our status as flawed creatures, not on the character
of God or the truth of His word. This isn't the place to articulate all our
doctrinal beliefs, but for the sake of transparency and accountability, we
do declare our belief in these basic tenets of Christianity:

- God is absolutely good.
- God is absolutely sovereign.
- Scripture is the inspired word of God and inerrant in its

original language.
- The one true God exists eternally in three persons: Father, Son, and Holy Spirit.
- Jesus Christ, the Son, was fully God and fully man.
- Jesus Christ lived a sinless life as a man on the earth.
- Jesus Christ died on a cross as a once-for-all sacrifice for sin, satisfying the righteous requirements of God and reconciling humankind to God.
- Jesus Christ rose bodily from the dead, ascended into heaven, and is seated at the right hand of the Father.
- Apart from Jesus Christ we are dead in our trespass and sin.
- By God's grace we are saved through faith in Jesus Christ; good works do not save us.
- Disciples of Jesus Christ are called to spread the gospel, obey His commands, and teach others to do the same.
- Jesus Christ will return to claim His bride, the Church.
- In the final judgment, satan and his demonic horde will be bound for eternity.[4]

How is this book organized?

Module 1: Foundational Concepts

We begin by discussing concepts we consider essential in our quest for greater freedom in Christ. They have helped us on our journey, and we believe they can help you, too. The more deeply we grasp and practice the truths presented in this module, the quicker and deeper our healing.

Modules 2-4: Truly Free, Legally Free, Practically Free

Truly, truly, I tell you, everyone who sins is a slave to sin. A slave is not a permanent member of the family, but a son belongs to it forever. So if the Son sets you free, you will be free indeed (John 8:34-36).

Modules 2-4 are organized around three ideas present in the phrase "free indeed." The first concerns truth. The second and third concern legalities and practicalities, respectively. First, the word "indeed" means "really and truly." To say we are free indeed is to emphasize that our freedom is real, true, and

---

4 We intentionally use a lowercase spelling of "satan" because we don't feel he deserves the honor of a proper noun.

attainable. So, in **Module 2** we discuss fundamental truths about ourselves and the freedom Christ offers. Living as slaves to sin is not inevitable. If we try to set ourselves free, we end up with counterfeit freedom, but the Son's freedom is real and true!

Next, in **Module 3**, we discuss what it means to be legally free based on Christ's finished work on the cross. We are free indeed because Christ paid for the deed which validates our freedom. A deed is a legal document signifying property ownership or legal rights. Jesus owns the deed to our freedom, and we can read the words of that deed in scripture. What's more, because we are co-heirs with Christ (Romans 8:17), we own the deed, too! In this module we discuss ways we may have forfeited our legal right to freedom and unpack how to make different choices so we can take back our freedom and the territory that is legally ours in Christ Jesus.

Finally, in **Module 4** we focus on the fact that our freedom is practical and doable! True freedom in Christ should affect our deeds—those actions that we take consciously and intentionally. Our behaviors don't have to be out of compulsion or habit anymore. It was for freedom that Christ has set us free. We can actually do it. If you are familiar with Paul's complaint in Romans 7, you may be wondering if it's true that we can really be freed in deed. Paul says, *For I have the desire to do what is good, but I cannot carry it out. For I do not do the good I want to do. Instead, I keep on doing the evil I do not want to do* (Romans 7:18b-19). It is tempting to read this and be consoled with the idea that even the Apostle Paul struggled with sin, so we shouldn't expect to do any better.

But Paul didn't stay stuck, and he doesn't expect us to stay stuck either. He is saying that on our own, we make a mess of it. *What a wretched man I am! Who will rescue me from this body of death?* (Romans 7:24). He answers his own rhetorical question immediately: *Thanks be to God, through Jesus Christ our Lord! [. . .] For in Christ Jesus the law of the Spirit of life set you free from the law of sin and death* (Romans 7:25, 8:2). God, through Jesus Christ, has done what we could not do for ourselves: We truly are free to live according to the Spirit. No matter how hard it may seem, we are free to live and act like we are free.

For it is God who works in you to will and to act in order to fulfill his good purpose (Philippians 2:13, NIV).

What's the process?

Real freedom isn't just about appearances or about preventing bad behavior. We can work on preventing outward, obvious sins by putting checks and balances in place to keep ourselves from doing stupid stuff—like not buying ice cream or not going to the bar after work or whatever. But self-management behaviors like these aren't the same thing as true freedom. As Paul told the church at Colossae, *Such regulations indeed have an appearance of wisdom, with their self-imposed worship, their false humility and their harsh treatment of the body, but they lack any value in restraining sensual indulgence* (Colossians 2:23, NIV). Self-management does nothing to address the root of our problems, which is usually a matter of the heart.

Because we cannot change the condition of our heart on our own, to be free **INDEED** requires that we partner with God the Father, Jesus Christ, and the Holy Spirit in the process. We elaborate and illustrate this process in the rest of this book, but it can be summarized with this acronym:

Identify
Need
Disagree
Evict
Exalt
Declare

First, we ask the Holy Spirit to **Identify** where, how, and why we are not free. We all have blind spots, and we need help to see what we need. If we ask in faith, the Holy Spirit will show us. He will not overwhelm us, but what He reveals He also gives grace to heal.

However, when the Spirit of truth comes, He will guide you into all truth. For He will not speak on His own, but He will speak what He hears, and He will declare to you what is to come (John 16:13).

If you continue in My word, you are truly My disciples. Then you will know the truth, and the truth will set you free (John 8:31b-32).

The second step in the process is to acknowledge our **Need** for God's grace. Whatever our sin or rebellious actions, we are already free from the penalty of that rebellion. Christ was nailed to a cross and pierced through His side on our behalf. Whatever our iniquities—our guilt, blameworthiness, and bent toward sin—he's already been crushed and bruised on our behalf. His punishment was for our peace, and His wounds were for our healing. Without Jesus, there is no real freedom. We need Him. If you are a Christian, then you already believe this and know it in your head. However, we don't always act as though we need Jesus. In Western, American culture, we are taught to be independent and self-sufficient. But in Kingdom culture, self-sufficiency is idolatry (worship of self over God), and it leads to spiritual bondage. Thus, we need to keep reminding ourselves that we need help!

For it is by grace you have been saved through faith, and this not from yourselves; it is the gift of God (Ephesians 2:8).

It is for freedom that Christ has set us free. Stand firm, then, and do not be encumbered once more by a yoke of slavery (Galatians 5:1).

From this place of humility and need, we can move to the third step in the process, which is to **Disagree** with the enemy and change our mindsets. To begin, you might need to disagree with the lie that you will never be free indeed. Disagree with the enemy's lie that you cannot get victory over your struggles. Disagree that it is too hard. Disagree that you deserve to be in bondage. Instead, ask for the faith to believe that God's grace and forgiveness is for you. Freedom, not slavery, is your inheritance in Christ.

Next, **Evict** the enemy. As you go through this book, the Holy Spirit will reveal areas that have caused bondage in body, soul, and/or spirit. We will explain Biblical, practical ways to evict the enemy: We can cast off darkness and be filled with the light of Christ. We can walk out of our prisons of guilt, shame, rejection, fear, etc. We can learn to resist the devil; he will flee and we'll be free.

Finally, to be free **INDEED** includes the choice to **Exalt** the Lord and **Declare** our allegiance to the truth. To exalt means to raise to a higher rank or position of power. Thus, to exalt the Lord means to acknowledge and agree with His higher rank and power compared to us and compared to any ungodly belief, any traumatic experience, or any deceiving spirits just evicted. Exalt also means to praise. It is so important that we not skip this step. The Psalmist declared that God inhabits the praises of His people (Psalm 22:3). He is pleased when we stand in awe and hope in His love (Psalm 147:11). Praise is good and pleasant and beautiful (Psalm 147:1). It also helps us keep our hearts humble and pliable rather than hard and resistant (Psalm 95:8).

You are my God, and I will praise you; you are my God, and I will exalt you. Give thanks to the Lord, for he is good; his love endures forever (Psalm 118:28-29, NIV).

Exalted be the LORD who delights in His servant's well-being (Psalm 35:27b).

Finally, we **Declare** the truths that replace whatever lies we once believed. We declare the truth that because Jesus sets us free, we are truly and legally free. We declare God's goodness. We declare our determination and commitment to the process of walking out our freedom without yielding ground back to the enemy. Please understand this step of declaration isn't New Age theology or a version of the "law of attraction."[5] Rather, this step involves the conscious choice to affirm God's truth and to remind ourselves out loud that we have been set free by His power alone. Declaring truth out loud is a way of getting that truth more firmly established in our hearts and minds. It also sends an unambiguous message to the prince of the "power of the air" (Ephesians 2:2), the devil, that we are sons and daughters of the King of Kings and our allegiance is to Him alone.

My mouth will declare Your righteousness and Your salvation all day long, though I cannot know their full measure. I will enter in the strength of the Lord GOD; I will proclaim Your righteousness—Yours alone (Psalm 71:15-16).

The people I formed for Myself will declare My praise (Isaiah 43:21).

---

5 The "law of attraction" is a New Age idea that positive thoughts and words have the energy and power to bring (attract) positive outcomes into our lives and negative thoughts and words have the power to attract negative outcomes. New Age and its law of attraction is a counterfeit, empty philosophy that denies the power of God and the gospel of Jesus Christ.

MODULE 1

FOUNDATIONAL CONCEPTS

As we begin to earnestly pursue greater freedom in Christ, it is useful to consider the goal. What should freedom look like? How should we think about ourselves, our current condition, our identity in Christ, and the process of growing up in the Lord? What truths will be most helpful for setting us free to glorify God and enjoy our relationship with Him? Should we expect to be miserable, or will there be joy in this journey?

All of us have sinned and fallen short of the glory of God (Romans 3:23). All of us are in need of saving, healing, and deliverance from the evil one. However, we won't dwell on our shortcomings. Instead, we begin this module by explaining that because our nature is multifaceted, we should expect the pursuit of freedom to be multifaceted as well.

Now may the God of peace Himself sanctify you completely, and may your entire spirit, soul, and body be kept blameless at the coming of our Lord Jesus Christ. The One who calls you is faithful, and He will do it (1 Thessalonians 5:23-24).

Spirit, Soul, and Body: What does freedom look like?

Christians believe in the eternal existence of God in three persons. He created us in His image (Genesis 1:27), and we, too, have three aspects: spirit, soul, and body. Because God is spirit (John 4:24), we are first and foremost spiritual beings. To a Western scientific mindset, this is nonsense. The church has been influenced by Cartesian dualism, which not only ignores our spiritual nature, but also separates "mind" and "body" rather than treating

10

individuals as whole beings with spirit, mind/will/emotions, and body. Furthermore, we have been socialized to believe in science and technology and to view with suspicion anything that we cannot readily explain and verify with our senses. But if we believe the Bible is true (and we do), then we must consider everything from the perspective that we are spiritual beings with a soul (mind, will, and emotions) housed in a body.

Some Christians have swung to the opposite extreme and focused primarily on spirit and subjective experience with less concern for reason or objective truth. The rise of New Age practices, which have significantly impacted American culture, is an example of this kind of extreme. Unfortunately, even in the church we often see that the pursuit of spiritual "experience" can get out of balance and result in Christians ignoring or being ignorant of sound biblical understanding and truth.

We need balance and alignment. Paul prayed that our whole "spirit, soul, and body" would be kept blameless until the day of Christ (1 Thessalonians 5:23). He understood that each of these aspects of our being is meant to operate in sync, not conflict, as God faithfully works to sanctify us through and through. It is tempting to treat the body as separate from the spirit or mind, and spiritual issues as separate from psychological ones. But as Neil Anderson points out in *The Bondage Breaker,* this approach is a mistake. Our spiritual, psychological (mind/emotions/will), and physical problems are intertwined. It is a mistake to ignore the interplay between spirit, soul, and body. It is also a mistake to ignore the spiritual dimension altogether just because we have a diagnosis of mental illness, neurodivergence, or some other disorder.

Spiritual truth is spiritually discerned. The Holy Spirit speaks to our spirit so that we may understand what God has freely given us in Christ (1 Corinthians 2:6-16). At the moment of salvation, our spirit was born again by the power of the Holy Spirit. We were given a new nature at conversion (see John 3:5-6; 2 Corinthians 5:17), and our spirits were made alive in Christ (Romans 8; Ephesians 2) by the power of the Holy Spirit. Yet we all know from experience that the new nature we received at salvation is not always perfectly expressed. Although we are seated with Christ in the heavenly places (Ephesians 2:6), our feet are sometimes stuck in the mud! Despite our positional sanctification (which we explain later in this module), we must grow, learn, and mature into our new character, identity, and calling in Christ. We do this through discipleship! We learn about who God is, His character, and His thoughts toward us by studying His love letters to us (the word of God). We grow through prayer, fellowship, and mentorship—being willing to learn from others who are more mature in their walk with Christ.

On this journey of progressive sanctification, we often experience inner conflict. We do not always behave consistently with the truth we know. One reason for this discrepancy is that our souls (mind, will, and emotions) are not replaced at the moment of salvation. We are still subject to habits of thought, feeling, and action. God doesn't erase our memories at the moment of salvation as if we were robots or computers. Instead, we are invited into the relational process of being transformed by the renewing of our minds (Romans 12:2). At salvation, we enter into a partnership with God, and He promises to be with us even as we learn to walk in His ways. As new creatures in Christ, we have a body that houses spirit and soul, including the Holy Spirit who now lives within us! Thus, we are exhorted to honor and glorify God with our bodies (see 1 Corinthians 6:19-20), treating them as holy just as He is holy. But we are working with pre-existing building materials, not necessarily new bricks and mortar.

Another reason we struggle is that our individualistic culture has elevated rationality and free will (independence) above other considerations, and we accept this idolatry as normal. Although free will and a sound mind are gifts from God, we are first and foremost spiritual beings made in the image of God. Is it any wonder we get confused and messed up when we try to reason our way into spiritual freedom? We cannot! As Paul expresses it, *The natural person does not accept the things of the Spirit of God, for they are folly to him, and he is not able to understand them because they are spiritually discerned* (1 Corinthians 2:14, ESV). Spiritual discernment and insight are not the same as rational understanding. We may come to understand later (see Module 2, "The Shelf of I Don't Know"), but if we limit our obedience only to what we can understand and control, we will continually struggle to be truly free. It feels a little scary to step outside the realm of rational understanding. It messes with our sense of control and predictability. But we can be sure that the peace of God—which quickly passes by our slow, puttering understanding—will guard our hearts and minds and keep us safely in Christ (Philippians 4:7).

When we are not in alignment as God designed us, with our born-again spirit leading the renewal of soul and body, we're in for trouble. If you are a "head person," you are led mainly by reason and analysis, and your feelings take a backseat in decision-making. If you are a "passionate" or "compassionate" person, you may let your emotions drive your behavior and decision-making. Or maybe you're just willful and stubborn, preferring to do things your way, even in situations where you know it's wiser or more pleasant to yield! In each case, misalignment results and true freedom is hindered. Each type of person operates primarily from the soul realm by allowing either the mind, emotions, or will to drive the bus. Of course, misalignment also results when we all, from time to time, allow the body to be in charge. Our physical flesh can and regularly does make a loud and compelling case that its needs and desires are the urgent priority, to the neglect of what is healthier for our soul and spirit.

The problem, of course, is God did not design us to function well when misaligned or unbalanced. If you are like us, there are times you need an adjustment. Just as a misaligned spine causes issues like pain, deformity, or immobility, so too spiritual misalignment causes problems like pain, a wrong or distorted perspective, fear, inaction, or wrong action. Both spinal and spiritual alignment depend on posture. We must position ourselves properly with Jesus as the head (Colossians 1:18). Our spirits, connected to the Holy Spirit, are to align under Christ (1 Corinthians 2:6-16) and then speak truth to our soul (mind, will, and emotions) and body. Spiritually, we can learn to be both upright and relaxed in our positional sanctification. We belong to Christ, and He has set us apart as His sons and daughters. He has set us free to enjoy His freedom (Galatians 5:1). We can stand firm in Him, refusing to be saddled with bondage or enslaved to fear, knowing that nothing can separate us from the Father's love (Romans 8:39).

At the same time, we can choose to exercise (discipline) ourselves unto godliness (1 Timothy 4:7). We know that with physical exercise, too much too soon leads to pain and injury. So also with spiritual discipline, treating ourselves harshly apart from the Holy Spirit's love and leading has no value in the long run (Colossians 2:23). So we continually ask the Lord to lead the quest, to identify what we need to do to cooperate with the kind intentions of His will and desire for our greater freedom and maturity. He is never harsh, and He is always wise. It is He who strengthens our inner being (Ephesians 3:16). His desire is that we be rooted and built up in Christ's love (Colossians 2:7), not that we perform or win some spiritual body-building contest.

So, freedom is multi-faceted (spirit, soul, and body), and the goal is to keep these aspects of our nature in their proper alignment. We tell our soul (mind, will, emotions) to listen to our spirit, which has been made new in Christ. King David gives us an example of what this looks like in Psalms 42 and 43 when he speaks to his soul and tells himself to hope in God. His spirit is taking authority over his circumstances, his mind, his emotions, and his will; he is commanding them all to align and yield to the truth that hope in God is never disappointed.

Why are you cast down, O my soul, and why are you in turmoil within me? Hope in God; for I shall again praise him, my salvation and my God (Psalm **43**:5, ESV).

In another song, David exhorts his soul to remember and rejoice in all the benefits of alignment:

Bless the LORD, O my soul, and all that is within me, bless his holy name! Bless the LORD, O my soul, and forget not all his benefits, who forgives all your iniquity, who heals all your diseases, who redeems your life from the pit, who crowns you with steadfast love and mercy, who satisfies you with good so that your youth is renewed like the eagle's (Psalm 103:1-5, ESV).

PRACTICAL APPLICATION

We will have more to say in Module 3 about taking thoughts captive to obey Christ (2 Corinthians 10:5), but now is a good time to remind ourselves that we need to stay aligned and in proper balance, spirit, soul, and body. Your spirit may need to wake up! Your mind may need to be retrained to focus on what is true. Your emotions may need to align with the truth, even if it takes a while. Be patient with yourself. Emotions aren't wrong (see Module 4), but they shouldn't be allowed to dictate your behavior. Remind your will that you have chosen to follow Christ, so there's no reason to be stubborn or defiant.

We offer the following prayer as one you may want to pray consistently for a while (perhaps daily for a week, a month, or even a year). Of course, feel free to put it in your own words:

Father, I choose right now to hope in your unfailing love. In the name of Jesus Christ, I tell any lingering unbelief, anxiety, or resistance to stop. I ask You, Holy Spirit, to awaken my spirit to receive grace where I so badly need it. I choose to believe Your word that nothing can separate me from the love of God in Christ Jesus. I choose to align my spirit, soul, and body with truth and to listen for Your loving, still small voice today, no matter the circumstances. Amen.

Along with this prayer (or something like it), we strongly recommend that you read Romans 8 every day. This chapter is full of truths that will change your life! In it we see the Triune God working on our behalf: God the

Father is working all things together for our good (verse 28). Jesus Christ is always interceding for us (verse 34). And the Holy Spirit is both helping us pray and interceding for us, too (verses 26-27)! Nothing can separate us from this great love (verse 39). We just need to keep reminding ourselves and meditating on the truth! You can also pray out the Psalms quoted earlier (Psalm 103:1-5, and Psalm 43:5) or any other scripture that you find refreshing and life-giving.

Identity and Worth: Who do you say I am?

As a professional illustrator, I (Sally) love beautifully illustrated children's books! Many years ago, on a cross-country vacation with my husband and young son, we happened upon a bookstore having a great sale, so we stocked up on new books for the drive. My son became particularly fond of a sweet book called *Small Brown Dog's Bad Remembering Day*. As I read this book over and over to my son, I had no idea how it would literally change my own life.

The story follows a little dog who wakes up one morning having forgotten who he is. On each page, he meets a dog who tells him something about himself, but no one can tell him his name. The story ends as the small brown dog goes to the police station where the police dog has his collar with his name on it. He rejoices to finally rediscover who he is. On the last page, the little mouse, which we see hidden on each page of the story, speaks for the first time and says, "But I could have told you that!"

While driving one day, I felt the Lord say, "Sally, you have become like Small Brown Dog. You have forgotten who you are."

I was an atheist when I was radically transformed by the love of God. I didn't seek Him when I was lost. Rather, He drew me and broke through my skepticism to show me how real He is and how deeply I am loved. He sought me when I was not looking and showered me with His love and healing. But somewhere along the way, that initial certainty in my spirit that I was fully loved had become weakened and twisted into a "bad remembering day." Like the cute little storybook dog, I had allowed others to define me. Fear of man and rejection had made me desperate for the approval of others, leading to neglect of the "still small voice" on every page of my life. He used this simple kids' story to invite me into a deeper understanding of His love and freedom. Like the mouse throughout the pages, always knowing who the small dog was, the "still small voice" of my Father reminded me to realign my heart with His and to seek Him for my identity. The old tapes of self-hatred, rejection, fear of man, worthlessness, etc., had been playing on repeat for so long that I truly did not know how to think any differently at that point. But He began to unpack my baggage and show me areas of trauma in my past that had created unhealthy mindsets and patterns of belief. He continues to remind me that my value and worth do not come from the approval of others but from seeing myself from God's perspective and who HE says I am. It has been a long journey but incredibly worthwhile.

From time to time, still, when I begin to allow anything other than the Father to define me, I am reminded of the story of a small brown dog, and I ask Him to turn my "bad remembering day" around.

PRACTICAL APPLICATION

Choosing God's perspective and believing who He says you are throughout scripture is key to recognizing and overcoming a "bad remembering day." The love of God is steadfast and immovable. His love never changes and never fails. We must continually choose to believe what God says about us over the enemy's lies and over our own fickle thoughts and emotions. The day God spoke to me about my "bad remembering day," I chose to listen to Him. Each day, I can choose His perspective or my own. To choose His perspective is an act of faith. There have been many times I have had to consciously remind myself, "I may have believed lies about myself in the past, but I know I have value and worth because the Lord says I do! I repent and renounce believing anything about myself that does not line up with God's word about me! He chose me! He died for me! In Christ I am free indeed!" If you, too, struggle with a sense of identity and worth, or if you want to strengthen yourself in the Lord, we have two suggestions and a prayer. Repeat them as necessary:

  • Read and ponder Ephesians 1:3-21 as often as it takes until you
    begin to see yourself as God sees you and are comfortable in your
    identity as beloved. We encourage you to search out the meaning
    of this passage using different translations. Invite the Lord to speak

to your heart through His word.

- Use your favorite music app or the internet to find the song "*Belovedness*" by Sarah Kroger. Read the lyrics. Listen on repeat until you begin to "own your belovedness."

Prayer

Father, thank You that I have been chosen by love from before the foundation of the world, according to Your word in Ephesians 1. Thank You that I have been adopted into Your eternal family. I am not alone or unloved, no matter what my feelings or my experiences tell me. Thank You that I am forgiven and redeemed by Your overflowing grace and mercy. Thank You that my identity as Your beloved is sealed and secured by the Holy Spirit who dwells in me and speaks to me words of affirmation, hope, identity, life, and purpose. Thank You that my past, my present, and my eternal future are in Christ alone. Open the eyes of my heart, Lord Jesus Christ, to see myself and others always through the lens of Your love. In Your name I pray. Amen.

Learning to See: Do I have the right perspective?

Because I (Sally) am an artist, God often helps me grasp truth through artistic concepts. My high school art teacher had a plaque on her wall that read, "Art is learning how to see." I have thought of that plaque often as I sought to look at things through new eyes, from new perspectives that bring beauty to the ordinary. Seeing from different perspectives brings insight. For many of us, our perspective is off or tainted, and we have problems seeing clearly any other way than how we have always seen. As the creator of everything, God sees more truly and more completely than we ever could. As we have experienced, freedom gets easier the more we see ourselves the way Jesus sees us and the more we taste of His goodness.

The dictionary offers many definitions of what it means "to see," and God has mastered them all! To see means:

- to perceive with the eyes; look at
- to perceive (things) mentally; discern; understand
- to understand intellectually or spiritually; have insight
- to give attention or care

17

- to find out; make inquiry
- to consider; think; deliberate
- see after, to attend to; take care of
- see out, to remain with (a task, project, etc.) until its completion
- see through, to penetrate to the true nature of; comprehend; detect
- to persevere: to see a difficult situation through

It is amazing to me that the God of all the universe truly sees us—He "sees through" to the very core of us! He "sees after, attends to, and takes care of" the task of working out our freedom until its completion. Our task is to agree with and allow Him to complete the masterpiece He sees in us without trying to pry the paintbrush out of His hand to do it our way.

Both in art and in our walk with the Lord, the angle at which we view things dramatically changes how we see them. Certain perspectives distort our perception. At certain angles the distortion can be so great that details are out of our line of sight, and it becomes very difficult to even make out what we are seeing. I always found it interesting to walk around the room after a life drawing session to see how different each artist's drawings could be simply because of where they were sitting in the room and how that changed their view. What objects were dominate in the drawings depended on where the artist sat and what was in their line of sight. What was front-and-center in one drawing may not even be visible in another. Yet each artist was looking at the same life drawing set up, just from differing angles.

When learning to draw, perspective is vitally important. A skillful use of perspective brings an image to life, whereas poorly drawn perspective can make an image look distorted and "off." The viewer may not be able to pinpoint the problem exactly, but it is obvious that something just isn't right.

18

WORM'S EYE VIEW
Horizon Line Perspective

- *Distorted view of self and others.*

- *Easily intimidated by others.*

- *Sees self as less than others or "below" them. Manifests as feelings of self-deprecation, second-guessing, self-consiousness, overthinking, and anxiety.*

A "worm's eye" view in art is used to portray a view from the ground looking up, like the view of a child looking up at a great big world. Or a bug ready to be smashed on the bottom of a shoe. This view can be used to create a feeling of awe or intimidation. Many of us have a "worm's eye" perspective of ourselves, and we can project that onto how we think God sees us. When we take this perspective, we may begin to feel "less than" others, smaller, inferior, self-conscious, easily intimidated, or afraid of being stepped on. This self-deprecating, woe-is-me perspective can make us feel like we are worthless and stuck in the dirt. We may have this view of ourselves because of rejection, the harsh and/or unkind words of others, and/ or the experience of being overlooked and feelings of being unwanted. Depression loves to taunt those who tend to see themselves from this perspective. But this isn't who we really are in Christ! God does not see us as worms, nor does He see others this way. True humility involves seeing ourselves as God sees us. Humility means to agree with God's perspective—to see and accept His love for us and to "penetrate to the true nature of and comprehend" the value He places on us. He sees us as worth the price of His son's death. False modesty/humility and the self-hatred that comes from seeing ourselves from a worm's eye perspective is a rejection of God's estimation of our worth. It's basically telling God that He is wrong. So a worm's eye view of ourselves is a crazy twisted form of pride!

As God's workmanship (Ephesians 2:10), we are His masterpiece! We may still be a work in progress, but He is faithful to complete what He starts!

For we are His workmanship [His own master work, a work of art], created in Christ Jesus [reborn from above—spiritually transformed, renewed, ready to be used] for good works, which God prepared [for us] beforehand [taking paths which He set], so that we would walk in them [living the good life which He prearranged and made ready for us] (Ephesians 2:10, AMP).

BIRD'S EYE VIEW

Horizon Line Perspective

- *Distorted view of self and others.*

- *Makes others feel intimidated.*

- *Sees self as "above" others. Manifests in pride, self-sufficiency, perfectionism, stubbornness, and over-confidence (to hide insecurity).*

A "bird's eye" perspective is looking down at a subject from high above. It can be used to show an expansive area, to make the subject look small or vulnerable, and to elicit a feeling of superiority. Like the worm's eye view, this perspective leads us to wrong thinking about ourselves and others. When we look down upon others from a bird's eye view, we can contribute to others feeling inferior or intimidated. This perspective is aloof, proud, and disconnected from those we deem "beneath us." This type of pride is prevalent in those prone to perfectionism and self-sufficiency. It's lonely in the loft! But in truth, just as with the "worm's eye" view, a "bird's eye" view of the world stems from insecurity and a failure to see ourselves as God sees us. We need Him to show us an undistorted view of ourselves that facilitates true humility, self-acceptance, and the security of knowing we are loved. When we see ourselves as He sees us, there is no need to look down on others.

Below on the left is a photo taken from a worm's eye view. The image on the right is the same subject from a bird's eye view. It is difficult to make out what the subject is because the extreme perspectives lack details and visual information.

Worm's Eye View   Bird's Eye View

NORMAL VIEW
Horizon Line Perspective

- *No distortion of view.*

- *Details lost in other perspectives are visible and clear.*

- *The "perspective" that God sees from is the* **ONLY true perspective** *free from distortion of self, others, or any other spiritual influences.*

"Normal view" in art is eye-level. In this perspective, details that may have been lost from other perspectives are now visible, and the viewer can make out what they are seeing without distortion. I think of the "normal view" perspective as an analogy of the right and true perspective that only God can give us. When we see ourselves and others from a right perspective, we neither elevate ourselves nor disparage ourselves relative to other people. God's perspective is free of distortion and wrong judgment. From His perspective, we are free to see our own and others' strengths and weaknesses with grace and love, to see the way God sees. We get God's perspective by seeing everything through His love and His word. God's word is the corrective lens to combat the distortion in our "seeing."

As you can see from the "bird's eye" and "worm's eye" images on page 22, the distortion from those extreme perspectives can make it hard to recognize even the most visited and recognizable iconic tourist attraction in the world. Yet seen from a "normal view" it is easy to make it out because it is no longer distorted.

Jesus told us in John 8:44 that the devil has no truth in him. He is a liar and the father of lies, so we know that whatever he tells us is twisted and cannot be right or trusted. The enemy is crafty and uses the trappings of truth to get us to believe lies about ourselves and God. The problem is that we often don't recognize it is the enemy speaking when we accept lies about ourselves, others, and even God.

You are of your father the devil, and it is your will to practice the desires [which are characteristic] of your father. He was a murderer from the beginning, and does not stand in the truth because there is no truth in him. When he lies, he speaks what is natural to him, for he is a liar and the father of lies and half-truths (John 8:44, AMP).

24

FORCED PERSPECTIVE

- *Using perspective to "trick" the mind.*

- *Truth is not always what we see!*

- *Certain perspectives can make what is **NOT** truth appear to be true.*

In art, "forced perspective" uses optical illusion to manipulate visual perception. Although sometimes in life it looks as though we have a good grasp on something, the devil loves to trick us into thinking that we understand ourselves and others and that we see all from the right perspective. But just as this picture obviously cannot represent the truth—no one can grasp the Eiffel Tower between their thumb and forefinger—we do not always see from the right perspective. Through smoke and mirrors, the enemy works to force his perspective into our thinking, influencing us to accept it as our own and to focus on what he wants us to see. He creates scenarios where small things are made to look huge and overwhelming, and the things that matter are diminished in our view. We need God to show us the truth and to reveal where satan has forced our perspective and tricked us into believing that lies are true or that truth is impossible.

Forced perspective only works when you look at a scene from a very narrow line of sight. Once you step to one side or the other, the illusion is broken as the truth of what you are seeing unfolds. In the picture on page 25, just a fraction of an inch to either side would ruin the illusion. Sometimes the issues of life and the flaws we see in ourselves or others are all that we seem to be able to focus on, and it can be difficult to step back and get true perspective. When the enemy has forced our perspective, making us see through a very narrow view, it is indicative of mindsets that need to be revealed, broken, and healed by the Father. God sees the whole picture and He reveals truth: *Then you will know the truth, and the truth will set you free* (John 8:32).

While editing this book, I had to put this principle into practice after I became focused on what I perceived as something unsavory in someone. In rereading this section, I realized I was not allowing God to show me His perspective. I was annoyed, and I had allowed that frustration to get me to agree with the enemy's "forced perspective," a perspective that is not truth! Am I willing to see from God's perspective and give up my "right" to see from my own? What if my perspective is not even really MY perspective at all, but one "forced" on me by the enemy? Do I want to allow the enemy to "force" his view into my thinking? NO!

Lord, help me to see with your eyes and with your heart of love! I CHOOSE to lay down the way I see myself and others, and I ask you to give me your perspective of myself and others.

DISTORTED PERSPECTIVE

MC Escher was a master of perspective, and his work illustrates its power. Escher frequently used artistic perspective to trick the mind. (You can view his art at https://mcescher.com). For example, the artwork above is a contemporary artist's take on Escher's work "Relativity." No matter how you turn the piece, the view seems "correct." You can't tell what is up or down. Looking closely, you can see the impossibility of the world that is depicted. In a similar manner, our enemy uses past wounds, traumas, misunderstandings, etc., to create distorted perspectives and impossible worlds. A master of perspective, he works to make us see through distorted lenses. He wants us to see ourselves and others in twisted ways.

Is it possible that you may be seeing yourself or others from a wrong perspective? From a perspective that may be tainted by woundedness or trauma? We believe that a huge step in our healing journey comes from the willingness to see truth from God's viewpoint, even if that perspective does not line up with our mindsets, experiences, or what we've always thought was true. Even if a different perspective seems impossible.

For example, many years ago I (Sally) was hurt very deeply by a situation that resulted in a huge financial loss for my family and myself, including the loss of our home. We had to live with friends for over a year, and the entire experience was extremely traumatic. A couple of years ago, while moving, I came across an old file containing legal documents and personal letters related to the situation. How this file had survived two cross-country moves and a fire in which we lost almost everything we owned is beyond me! But the Lord had a huge lesson in it for me. As I looked through the file all those years later, with a heart more healed, I realized how much my perspective had changed. Although the evidence still shows that we suffered a real injustice and had valid reasons for the hurt, many of the little things that I remembered as part of the situation were not actually grounded in fact. My memory had distorted the picture so that the "villain" was completely wrong, and I was completely innocent. From my more healed perspective, I could see in the letters I'd written that my response to the injustice fell far short of the untainted righteousness I remembered having! Reading that file really opened my eyes to the ways memories can be misconstrued by woundedness and self-serving defensiveness. Our memories are not video recorders. What we remember can be influenced by our current attitudes, beliefs, and feelings![6] When the dominant feeling is hurt and anger, our "memories" will tend to justify and amplify those feelings.

Interestingly, memory and psychological defenses can work in the opposite way as well. We can distort the truth and dampen or "forget" what we want to forget. I have a dear friend who had convinced himself that his past was not a big deal. He did not want to believe that his childhood trauma or the emotional pain of an absent father was affecting him in the present. Af-

---

6 Schacter, D. L. (2022). The seven sins of memory: An update. *Memory, 30*(1), 37-42.

ter attending one of our Free INDEED classes, the Lord began shifting his perspective. He began to see how deep the hurt actually went and how much it was affecting his adult life and choices. His eyes and heart were opened, and he is now walking through the healing process and gaining more and more emotional and spiritual freedom!

Our perspective is also influenced by our physical condition because we are spirit, soul, and body. Studies of embodied cognition show the connection between our physical state and our perceptual and mental processes. For example, people perceive a hill as steeper and a backpack as heavier when they are physically tired compared to when they are not tired.[7] In other words, our perception of reality, our perspective, is influenced by our physical state. The enemy loves to exhaust and deplete us anyway he can. Sometimes "spiritual warfare" can simply mean choosing to put down the phone or turn off the television in favor of going to bed! We focus mostly on taking care of spirit and soul, but we encourage you to take care of your body, too. As you work your way through this material, remember that you need to move your body, to get enough rest, and eat food that will nourish you. It matters, and you matter!

PRACTICAL APPLICATION

We encourage you to take some time in prayer and private reflection to ask the Lord to show you His perspective. Allow Him to identify a specific way in which your perspective might be off. Are you seeing yourself, others, circumstances, or challenges the way He does? If not, say a quick prayer of repentance and ask God to show you His perspective.

And if the practical, bodily side of "perspective" needs adjustment—if you need to get more rest, more exercise, better nutrition, or whatever— then invite the Lord to help you with specific action steps. Let Him encourage your mind and heart and influence your will to make better choices (e.g., adding a daily serving of veggies, walking 15 minutes tomorrow, going to bed 15 minutes earlier than yesterday). We pray for you as the apostle John did for His friend Gaius: *Beloved, I pray that in every way you*

---

7 Proffitt, D. R. (2006). Embodied perception and the economy of action. *Perspectives on Psychological Science, 1*(2), 110-122.

may prosper and enjoy good health, as your soul also prospers (3 John 1:2).

We know that the freedom road can seem daunting and overwhelming at times. We want to remind you that God sees you and loves you right where you are and will walk you through! For us, freedom has come in layers, one layer at a time, as the Lord walked us through. He desires for you to be free of every hindrance weighing you down to run your race, and He is faithful to do the work as you submit to His process. You can trust Him.

Therefore, since we are surrounded by such a huge crowd of witnesses to the life of faith, let us strip off every weight that slows us down, especially the sin that so easily trips us up. And let us run with endurance the race God has set before us (Hebrews 12:1, NLT).

Focus and Mindset: Do I need to see differently?

To look closely at the famous Georges Seurat painting, "A Sunday Afternoon on the Island of La Grande Jatte," is like looking at a pixelated screen of seemingly meaningless dots. But when you enter the room of the Art Institute of Chicago where is hangs and see it from a distance, the beauty and vibrancy of a warm summer day in Paris in the 1880's comes to life. The piece is stunningly beautiful, and no photographs do it justice. It has to be experienced in person to fully appreciate it. The artist used a technique called pointillism, which uses small dots of paint to create patterns and images. Up close, these paint points don't look like much of anything. A single dot or an isolated cluster of dots doesn't convey much meaning. Same with us. When we are in the middle of our messy lives, we can't see what the Artist sees or what he's working on. Only He truly sees the whole picture and knows the purpose and point of apparently random points of life. I am amazed at how Seurat was able to envision how those small dots would translate into the scene he created on that huge canvas. I have wondered how many times he had to step back to see how it was coming together and not hyperfocus on any particular dot. When we stand back and look at the bigger picture of our lives, we begin to see beauty in the whole picture. A gifted painter was able to create a masterpiece that fascinates and delights as we see the mosaic of tiny points of paint become a glorious scene. How much more glorious it is to learn to trust the Master—and to trust Him that one day we will be able to step back and see the whole picture. He makes beauty out of ashes and brings joy into our places of despair (Isaiah 61).

What do you see in the above picture? Two faces? A vase? Both are there, and whatever you see first makes it more difficult to see the other. This illusionary effect was used by MC Escher in many of his works including "Heaven and Hell." In that work, there are black bat-like demons and white angels interwoven within a circle. Looking at that image, the figures you see first will dominate (say the demons), and it takes great effort to see the other figures (the angels). When we have viewed ourselves (or others) from one perspective for a long time, it can be very difficult to see anything else. It takes an act of our will to *decide* to shift our focus from what dominates our sight. Similarly, we can ask for God's help to shift our focus and change how we see ourselves, others, and our circumstances to how He sees them. The more we grow in freedom, the more we desire to focus on what God sees—free from filters brought on by traumas, painful distortions and outright lies—and to shift focus to the light and away from the darkness.

As a child, I (Sally) learned to hate beets. I hated everything about them, from their earthy smell (like dirt and rotting leaves) to the fact that they stain every-thing they touch. Growing up, I figured nothing could change my mind. I was determined, obstinate, and completely closed-minded on the subject of beets. But I also love all things food, and I am a huge fan of clean, healthy eating. So, a couple of years ago, after reading yet another article on the nutritious benefits of beets, I opened my mind enough to admit that it had been many years since I had actually tried one. For the first time since childhood, I put pride down long enough to consider the thought that I could be wrong about beets.

From the moment I decided to give beets a second chance to win me over, I saw them as a culinary challenge! I was going to show myself, as I have shown many friends who had been averse to other healthy foods, that the right cooking method, spices, and food pairings can completely change our opinion of foods. After searching out many recipes and setting out with an open mind, my view of beets as the most gag-worthy vegetable in existence began to change. To my own shock and amazement, I discovered I could actually enjoy them! If you are a fellow beet hater, you may have a hard time believing the best about beets. But I have learned to love them and appreciate their bold, red color and their nutrition-packed benefits. I have also changed the minds of other beet haters with the recipes I have developed. Oh, taste and see that a beet is good!

So, do I digress? What do beets have to do with freedom? Well, much of our life in Christ—and the struggles we face—are about mindsets. I had the mindset of a lifelong beet hater. I thought that if I had to eat them, they were going to be awful. It was a mindset and attitude that had become so entrenched that I didn't think it possible to change. But I was basing my aversion to this nutritional powerhouse on a taste I'd experienced so long ago that I couldn't even tell you when or where I'd had that experience! As an adult, I know that food that is good for you doesn't need to taste bad. Good food cooked right is life-giving and energizing. Obviously, we need the right nutrients for our bodies to function at their best. But we still have a hard time eating enough fruits and vegetables and trimming the junk out of our diet. We often have the mindset that good food doesn't taste good, that the joy is in the junk. Not only that, but we also like the convenience of junk food. Beets can't be ordered in a drive through (thank God). The speed and ease with which we can eat junk food keeps us coming back to it. And, quite frankly, we are sometimes too lazy to prepare a good, nutritious meal. Sometimes being a Christian can feel like eating badly prepared beets. Or like subsisting on a diet of raw carrots and celery while watching everyone else in the world eat luscious chocolate cake. When we get tired of the work of chopping unappetizing raw veggies, we hit the drive through and binge on junk. We have a mindset problem. But God challenges us to "taste and see that the Lord is good" (Psalm 34:8). So many of us are like beet haters— stuck in an unhealthy mindset because of past experiences of hurt and disappointment. We let the bad taste in our mouth dictate our current response. Perhaps you tried opening your heart to someone and they hurt you. Like an avowed beet hater, you vowed never to open yourself up like that again. "Danger! You'll hate this. It hurt you in the past and will hurt you again." Or perhaps the bad taste in your mouth concerns church. Been there, done that. Never gonna step inside the First Church of Canned Beets ever again.

Understandable.

But what if we tried, from an adult perspective, to taste and see again? What if God, like beets, really is good? Are we willing to consider that maybe, just maybe, our perceptions can be changed or that our mindsets need adjusting? Maybe what was fed to us in the past was broken. Or cold. Or canned. Maybe we've been force-feeding ourselves beets or raw celery and carrots, spiritually speaking, because we knew they were "good for us." But what would happen to our relationship with God if we actually believed and experienced that He is good like chocolate, not just good for us like beets?

Maybe Daddy God wants to sit us down for a feast! He wants us to enjoy our life with Him, not just choke down what's good for us or pretend to eat (all the while spitting into a napkin when no one is looking). He wants us to know His love and be free to reciprocate that love without the stench of obligation, duty, or pretense. He wants you to taste and see that He is good! Carrots can be amazing in many ways...roasted and glazed or in carrot cake, etc. Beets can actually enrich a chocolate cake! Likewise, maybe He wants to transform those things that we have stubbornly held onto, those old mindsets and defense mechanisms, and make something beautiful and good!

The Prodigal Son/Loving Father: What is my perspective of the Father?

God loves us so much that He would rather die than live without us. He wanted to regain the intimacy lost in the Garden of Eden when Adam and Eve ate the forbidden fruit. Redemption means to regain something by payment or clearing a debt. Although the debt of sin was not His, He paid the penalty (death) to regain connection. Rather than abandon us to our lost and sinful state, He chose to give His one and only son, Jesus, to die on a cross as a redeeming sacrifice. This is Christianity 101. This is how He loves.

The parable of the prodigal son/loving father (Luke 15:11-32) illustrates this extravagant love. It is a familiar parable to many of us, but we want to take a fresh look, applying what we've learned about perspective. As we do, we ask the Father to give you fresh revelation, eyes to see something new that will touch your heart with His love.

Then Jesus said, "There was a man who had two sons. The younger son said to him, 'Father, give me my share of the estate.' So, he divided his property between them. After a few days, the younger son got everything together and journeyed to a distant country, where he squandered his wealth in wild living. After he had spent all he had, a severe famine swept through that country, and he began to be in need. So he went and hired himself out to a citizen of that country, who sent him into his fields to feed the pigs. He longed to fill his belly with the pods the pigs were eating, but no one would give him a thing.

Finally he came to his senses and said, 'How many of my father's hired servants have plenty of food? But here I am, starving to death! I will get up and go back to my father and say to him, "Father, I have sinned against heaven and against you. I am no longer worthy to be called your son. Make me like one of your hired servants."' So he got up and went to his father. But while he was still in the distance, his father saw him and was filled with compassion. He ran to his son, embraced him, and kissed him. The son declared, 'Father, I have sinned against heaven and against you. I am no longer worthy to be called your son.' But the father said to his servants, 'Quick! Bring the best robe and put it on him. Put a ring on his finger and sandals on his feet. Bring the fattened calf and kill it. Let us feast and celebrate. For this son of mine was dead and is alive again! He was lost and is found!' So they began to celebrate.

Meanwhile the older son was in the field, and as he approached the house, he heard music and dancing. So he called one of the servants and asked what was going on. 'Your brother has returned,' he said, 'and your father has killed the fattened calf, because he has him back safe and sound.' The older son became angry and refused to go in. So his father came out and pleaded with him. But he answered his father, 'Look, all these years I have served you and never disobeyed a commandment of yours. Yet you never gave me even a young goat so I could celebrate with my friends. But when this son of yours returns from squandering your wealth with prostitutes, you kill the fattened calf for him!' 'Son, you are always with me,' the father said, 'and all that is mine is yours. But it was fitting to celebrate and be glad, because this brother of yours was dead and is alive again; he was lost and is found'" (Luke 15:11-32).

The father here represents our Heavenly Father. This parable reveals so much about His heart toward us. When we look with the right perspective, we can see the following dimensions of God's goodness and love:

- Understanding—he knows his sons and what they truly need.
- Generosity—all that was his was theirs.
- Wisdom
- Love—the kind that gives us freedom to choose.
- Compassion
- Protection—the father ran, which was unseemly for a man of his age and standing to do in that culture. It was also shameful as he would have had to gird up his robes to run. By running, he protected his son's heart, taking the shame and attention of gawkers onto himself and drawing it away from his son.
- Mercy—he had the legal right to reject his son, but he forgave him instead.
- Hope/patience—he must have been looking for his son regularly because he saw him from a long way off.
- Affection—he embraced and kissed his son immediately, even before he'd bathed.
- Hopeful expectation—he was prepared to give his son a ring, sandals, and a robe that fit! He was expecting the son's return.
- Attention to detail—he knows every intricate detail of who we are…he apparently knew his son's ring and shoe size.

The father in this parable (and by extension our Heavenly Father) is not angry, judgmental, or grudge-bearing. He delights to restore us and give us back our identity and position as sons and daughters. His love is lavish, free, and given without strings attached. His joy and willingness to celebrate our return, no matter how far we have strayed or how long we have been gone, is genuine and unreserved. No matter what we do or fail to do, God is faithful, patient, kind, and good.

May we deepen our belief in God's character and our trust in His goodness. He wants a connection with us more than anything. Our freedom depends on us believing that He is good—a belief that is more than just mental assent to the concept of a good God. We need to have our entire spirit, soul, and body in agreement with the notion that God is good. Many Christians do believe it with their minds but remain unconvinced in their hearts.

35

Often, negative experiences appear to contradict that truth. We will have more to say about this vital issue in Module 2, but there is no time like the present to ask for a deeper revelation of His goodness and love.

This parable also shows us two sons with very different but both quite wrong ideas about their father and their own identity/position as sons.

The "Prodigal" Son's Entitled Worm's Eye Perspective

A close look at the "prodigal" son's behavior reveals a distorted, worm's eye perspective. He assumed he would have no long-term place of value in the family business. We can hear him thinking, "My brother is going to get the best of the inheritance and pass it on to his kids. I might as well take what I can get now and leave. I'm not worthy of anything more than second-best." How he sees his father, himself, and his place in the family business is off. By selfishly and disrespectfully demanding his inheritance, he acted as though his father was already dead. What a twisted view he had of himself and his father. His actions show his immaturity, his idolatry (wanting money more than family unity), and his self-indulgence. Only when he runs out of money and some semblance of self-respect does he decide to return to his father. Even so, he plans to return in a way that is self-punishing— from a worm's eye perspective—not expecting to be loved or welcomed home. He left feeling unloved and undervalued, and now he expects to be treated like a hired hand, not even like a family member.

The Older Son's Sullen Bird's Eye Perspective

Now consider the older son. His perspective was also distorted, but given his brother's shameful behavior, he takes the proud, lofty view. He, too, fails to understand the father's love. He behaves like an orphan even though he has access to all his father owned. He is angry, judgmental, proud, self-righteous, unloving, jealous, sullen, and insecure.

He presumes to know his father's attitude toward the younger brother, and he is proud that he is not like his brother. He believes his good behavior and obedience should be rewarded, and his brother's profligate behavior should be punished rather than celebrated with the best calf on the farm. In pride and self-righteousness, he points out that he never disobeyed a command. Then he blames the father for never giving him a thing; he feels he deserves a praise party, not his rogue brother. He is so angry and offended at his father's behavior toward the returned son that he refuses to go inside where the celebration is happening.

Pride can be a subtle snare, but when we let ourselves get deceived into thinking that our "good behavior" somehow earns us the right to a place at the Father's banqueting table, we effectively tell Jesus that His sacrificial death on the cross wasn't necessary. When we try to be self-sufficient or believe that we can improve upon Christ's finished work, then we totally miss the whole point of the Christian faith—which is that there is nothing we can do to earn God's love or improve upon Jesus' sacrifice for sin. Jesus became sin for us so that we might be called God's children and live in His presence and know His favor. We did not earn it and cannot improve upon this free gift of life. Even if our behavior is more "righteous" than the next guy (like the older son imagining his behavior to be more virtuous than his brother's), that doesn't mean our righteous behavior is good enough; it is not and never can be. Social comparison may make us feel better about ourselves, but it does nothing to raise our standing with God.

Passivity is another element of the older brother's behavior. When the father is surprised by his son's attitude, his response is to point out that everything he has belongs to the son. Although it's not explicit in the passage, we think the father is essentially saying, "Son, you never asked for a calf or a party or anything. All you had to do was say you wanted to have a party with your friends, and it would have been fine! All I have is yours. No one ever stopped you from having a party with your friends. You shouldn't blame me. You never took the initiative to ask."

And why not? Because the older son presumed to know what his father would say if he asked for a party. He did not know the heart of his father, who would have delighted to have his son be happy and celebrating with friends. But the son sees the father as all business and no pleasure and therefore unlikely to say yes. Rather than risk rejection or risk making his father unhappy with him, he "suffers in silence." He never asks for anything because he thinks he knows what will happen. He prefers false humility and playing the martyr to risking an honest conversation with his father. He no more knew his dad than the younger brother did!

How often do we rob ourselves of happiness by presuming we know how others will respond to us or how God will treat us? Pride and presumption partner with self-sufficiency but leave us unhappy. Solomon saw the lonely danger of self-sufficiency in his ecclesiastical musings and contrasted it with the blessing of community and interdependence:

Again, I saw futility under the sun. There is a man all alone, without even a son or brother. And though there is no end to his labor, his eyes are still not content with his wealth: "For whom do I toil and bereave my soul of enjoyment?" This too is futile—a miserable task.

Two are better than one, because they have a good return for their labor. For if one falls down, his companion can lift him up; but pity the one who falls without another to help him up! Again, if two lie down together, they will keep warm; but how can one keep warm alone? And though one may be overpowered, two can resist. Moreover, a cord of three strands is not quickly broken (Ecclesiastes 4:7-12).

We can just hear the older son asking himself, "Why have I worked so hard all these years, depriving myself of fun while my brother is off living it up? Now he has the audacity to come back, and my father throws him a party? It's not fair!" The older son is evidently toiling alone, unaware of his father's true love. He thinks he knows his dad, but he doesn't. And all those years of toiling were vanity and an unhappy business because he missed the point—that everything that belonged to the father belonged to him. He could have been living in happy connection with his father. Instead, he's toeing the line, doing all the right things, going it alone without his father's help or input and missing the point completely.

The "horizon line/normal perspective" of the Christian life shows us the Father's loving devotion to His children. Nothing we do or don't do can change the nature and reality of His love for us. This is the basic truth of the Christian faith: Everything—even our very life and breath—depends upon it. In Module 2 we will dive a little deeper into God's love because the more clearly we see it and receive it, the easier it gets to truly live and walk in the freedom for which Christ has set us free. As we continue this journey, may we grow in the revelation that He has already chosen us and loves us with absolute and unchangeable faithfulness.

PRACTICAL APPLICATION

What is your view of yourself and God? Is your perspective distorted? We ask that the eyes of your heart be open to seeing yourself as He sees you (Ephesians 1:18). May you come to know and believe the truth of who you are in Christ and to see yourself as the Father sees you. He loves you with an everlasting love, and He is always rejoicing over you with singing (Zephaniah 3:17). If you find it difficult to receive love and affirmation, that's okay. The Father doesn't disapprove. He is patient in the process as you grow in faith and love. We pray that what we share both here and in the pages to come will help you grow in your ability to hear His voice and freely receive His love and transformative grace.

If you've never learned about (or are out of practice) hearing the voice of God, first believe that you can hear Him. Jesus promised that His sheep know and hear His voice (John 10:27). The fact that you are a born-again believer is proof that you heard the voice of the Good Shepherd and responded to His call. Sometimes He speaks in a whisper, a still small voice we perceive in our spirit (1 Kings 19:12). Other times, His voice is like the sound of many waters (Revelation 1:15)! Every time, without fail, He speaks truth in love. He never says anything that contradicts scripture or the law of love. That is why we cannot overemphasize the importance of scripture. Each one of us can hear Him speak as we read and study His word. It teaches us His character and His ways. Scripture is a guardrail that keeps us on the track of truth. It is guidance, wisdom, and loving correction. It contains love poetry, comfort, and peace. His word speaks. May our hearts listen and receive.

In addition to allowing God to change your perspective through the study of His word, we pray also that you will grow in intimacy through prayer.

But you, beloved, building yourselves up in your most holy faith and praying in the Holy Spirit (Jude 1:20, ESV).

Likewise the Spirit helps us in our weakness. For we do not know what to pray for as we ought, but the Spirit himself intercedes for us with groanings too deep for words (Romans 8:26 ESV).

Praying in the Spirit is a powerful way to grow in faith and learn to hone our sensitivity to what He is saying. We have found that when we pray in the Spirit, the Father speaks to our hearts, encourages us, and gives us direction (Ephesians 6:18). If you pray in tongues, we suggest committing to seeking Him in this way regularly as you continue this freedom journey (1 Corinthians 14:14-15). If you do not yet have a prayer language, ask the Holy Spirit! You can also ask a trusted friend to pray with you.

Sanctification: Should growing up in the Lord be a bummer?

Remarkably, even though the two sons in the parable of the prodigal had an amazing father, neither one truly understood his heart! That fact is both fascinating and comforting. Even with the greatest parents on the planet, children develop misperceptions and misunderstandings that take time, effort, and increasing maturity to correct. In other words, it is necessary for us to let go of our childish perceptions (1 Corinthians 13:11). As we mature in our faith, we will begin to walk in greater levels of freedom. There is no microwave maturity.

Growing up in our faith is called sanctification. It means to be set apart or made holy. Pursuing sanctification can seem hard, intimidating, mysterious, joyless, or even impossible. Frankly, such a view comes from a religious, Pharisaical mindset. This mindset considers self-effort as more important and effective than God's power at work in us. But God doesn't expect us to make ourselves "right" or "clean" before Him. Only Jesus' blood can wash away our sin and make us whole again. But how easy it is to be influenced by this lie designed to steal our joy and poison our relationship with Father God. We want to show you that when we understand the Father's heart and the true meaning of sanctification, the idea isn't nearly as scary, intimidating, or awful as we may have thought!

The word "sanctify" (also translated "make holy") means "to set apart" for God. In general, something is sanctified when it is intentionally set apart for its intended use. A guitar is sanctified when used to play music, but not so much when used to irritate a roommate. A pen is sanctified when used to write, a cup when used to hold liquid, and a car when used for transportation. Likewise, we are sanctified when we are fulfilling our purpose and doing what we were designed to do. So, what is our purpose? The Westminster Catechism states that humanity's chief end is to "glorify God and enjoy Him forever." Thus, we are living a sanctified life when our choices bring glory to God and when we are enjoying our relationship with Him! That doesn't mean we don't make mistakes or get dirty. It does mean that we acknowledge God's absolute holiness and allow Him to cleanse and change us. What is a healthy and helpful view of sanctification? My (Sally's) understanding changed radically one night at a prayer group. As we began to pray for someone, I got a picture in my mind of him as a little boy, immersed to the chest in a bathtub overflowing with bubbles. He was having a blast. I prayed out, "You are in a bubble bath, and your Daddy is there. And there are bubbles and toys, and it's fun! And you are being sanctified..."

When I said that, I felt the revelation hit like a tsunami: Sanctification is like a bubble bath! I was seeing this man as a little boy, having a blast in a bubble bath, spending quality time with his Daddy. They were having so much fun! Children hardly notice they are getting clean during a bubble bath. The focus is togetherness and fun! Somewhere I had picked up the idea that to be sanctified and holy meant I had to do everything right. It was more like being scrubbed with a wire brush than soap and bubbles. But that night I saw that sanctification means bath time with my heavenly Daddy. It involves freedom, love, and the enjoyment of His company.

Can you see your heavenly Father from this perspective—as the best Dad ever giving His kid a bubble bath? A good father doesn't get irrationally angry when his kids get dirty. But he does make sure they get clean. He doesn't leave them alone in the tub because that is dangerous, and they could drown. Nor does he just sit there looking at them with stern judgment waiting for them to use the washcloth properly. No. A good father plays at the edge of the tub with his kids, enjoying the process, blowing bubbles, dive-bombing the rubber ducky, singing silly songs, and laughing—all while making sure they are clean before climbing out and getting ready for bed.

That said, let's consider three types of sanctification. When we come to Jesus, at the moment of salvation, we are given positional sanctification. We are "in Christ" and immediately set apart for God. In Christ we are made holy and righteous (given right standing with God) because of what Jesus did for us. We didn't earn this right position with God, and we don't deserve it. We are in Christ Jesus, *who became for us wisdom from God—and righteousness, and sanctification, and redemption* (1 Corinthians 1:30, NKJV). As believers in Jesus Christ, we have positional sanctification whether we know it and enjoy it or not! A second type is called experiential (or progressive) sanctification. Just as it sounds, this type of sanctification refers to the progression and experience of growing in the Lord. It refers to growing in spiritual maturity and becoming more like Jesus. "Bubble bath" sanctification is this experiential/progressive type of sanctification. As we spend time with our Daddy and learn from His word, we develop character and grow in wisdom. We become better able to fulfill our purpose and be used as He intended. Lastly, there is ultimate (or complete) sanctification which refers to the glorification that takes place at Jesus' second coming. *When Christ, who is your life, appears, then you also will appear with Him in glory* (Colossians 3:4).

Looking again at the prodigal son/lovesick father, we can see that the older brother had positional sanctification; he was working for his father and in his purpose. But he did not have experiential sanctification because he didn't understand his identity as a son or his purpose in the family business. He needed a bubble bath! He shows no signs that he enjoyed experiencing his position as a son. Instead, he worked and served out of obligation. We see this because of his angry and jealous response. Hearts that know who and whose they are do not respond in jealousy or anger when Father God loves another one of His kids. On the part of the younger son, his father was overjoyed that he returned; he was quick to restore him back to his position as a son. The father made sure he got cleaned up (bubble bath) and properly clothed. The younger son came back into his purpose and identity, and so we see him receiving both positional sanctification and experiential sanctification—to the great joy of his father.

PRACTICAL APPLICATION

Christ loved the church and gave himself up for her, that he might sanctify her, having cleansed her by the washing of water with the word (Ephesians 5:25b-26, ESV).

Take a few moments to think about the sanctification process (specifically, experiential/progressive sanctification). Do you easily embrace the "bubble bath" view, or do you resist that picture for some reason? Why? Are you quick to yield to bath time, or do you tend to resist? If for any reason you feel uncomfortable with the process, that is a clue that deeper healing and freedom is needed. Be encouraged to stay in the process! Getting more freedom doesn't have to be miserable! The one who calls you to be sanctified body, soul, and spirit is faithful, and He will do it (1 Thessalonians 5:23-24)!

Iniquity: What about when I mess up?

Some Christian concepts (like sanctification or repentance) can sound intimidating. If you've grown up in the church, these terms may be so familiar as to have lost any meaning (if they ever had any for you). In our experience, "Christianese" language without understanding doesn't set people free. However, things change when the Lord gives a fresh perspective, like He did with sanctification and the bubble bath! There is so much freedom in seeing how He sees. So it is with the final basic concept we want to discuss: iniquity. For a good part of my Christian walk, I (Sally) thought the terms sin, trespass, transgression, and iniquity were pretty much interchangeable. Turns out they are quite different, and those differences matter. Understanding them makes our choices a little clearer. The better equipped we are to choose wisely—in ways that move us toward God rather than away from him—the swifter our growth and the deeper our freedom.

So now, let's look at these terms:

*I acknowledged my **sin** to You, and my **iniquity** I did not hide. I said, I will confess my **transgressions** to the Lord [continually unfolding the past till all is told]—then You [instantly] forgave me the guilt and iniquity of my sin. Selah [pause, and calmly think of that]* (Psalm 32:5, AMPC).

The bolded terms in this verse have similar meanings but are not exact synonyms. Each term refers to a type of lawlessness, but to varying degrees. A progression is revealed when you take a closer look:

Sin (*chââ'*) is an archery term meaning to "miss the mark." It can mean a mistake, doing the wrong thing unwittingly, or failing to do what is right. The mistake is not necessarily intentional, but it is wrong nonetheless.

Trespass (*maal*) refers to an unfaithful or treacherous act. It is intentional. To commit a trespass is to know something is wrong and choose to do it anyway.

Transgression (*pesha*) means a revolt or rebellion. It involves intentionally choosing to disobey or disregard legitimate authority. A transgression is an intentional refusal to accept or do what is right. So, a transgression is more than a mistake or a trespass because it is done in defiance of authority.

Iniquity (*âvôn*) is a term that means twisted, crooked, bent, or distorted. Iniquity involves twisted, perverse thinking. Iniquity is a term used to express the wicked, unholy condition of the heart resulting from repeated, unrepented

43

sin, trespass, and transgression.

Here is a helpful analogy about the differences among these terms: Imagine walking down the road and seeing your friends out in a field. They call you to join them, so you do. When you get out into the field, you see "No Trespassing" signs in the field you just crossed. The signs were facing the opposite direction, and you did not see them until you turned around. You did not know you were trespassing on the property, so for you it was a mistake, a sin (unintentional wrongdoing). However, if you decided to walk across the field another day, you would know you were trespassing. The proper term for that choice is trespass (a known wrongdoing). If you decide to walk across that field even as the owner of the land tries to stop you, you are now rebelliously disregarding the law. Your behavior now is a trans-gression (a defiant and rebellious wrongdoing). Finally, your friends' behavior qualifies as iniquity because they knew they were breaking the law, and they enticed you to break it, too. They intentionally acted as though they were above the law, rebelliously disregarding it and inviting you into their lawless behavior.

Although these distinctions may seem minor, they are important in our quest for greater freedom and maturity. A simple mistake, a sin, is very different from the choice (or repeated choices) to continue in it (progressing from trespass to transgression to iniquity). God, through Jesus Christ, can and does forgive us the guilt of all of these. But when we choose to move in rebellion, when we make the choice to do what we know is wrong, then we are opening the door to iniquity. Continuing in trespass and transgression leads to iniquity and bondage because it gives the enemy the legal right to torment us. (We will come back to this issue in Module 3, where we discuss how to shut the door to the enemy and reclaim our legal right to freedom in Christ.)

PRACTICAL APPLICATION

Perfect, mistake-free living is an impossible goal. We all miss the mark and mess up. One of the best ways to apply what we've learned in this section about sin, trespass, transgression, and iniquity is to confess as soon as possible. There is no shame in making mistakes. Trying to hide them can be a slippery slope into bondage and iniquity. But if we confess our sin, God forgives and cleanses us and chooses not to hold our sins against us (1 John 1:9). Confession and repentance are discipleship habits that we need to learn and practice on our road to freedom—by confessing regularly in prayer to the Lord and by confessing one to another (James 5:16).

In addition to the practice of confession and repentance, we suggest that you take the time to look up and prayerfully read each of the following passages. If you are keeping a spiritual journal, you may find it beneficial to write out one or more of these and/or memorize them.

- 1 John 1:7-9
- James 5:16
- Psalm 19: 7-14
- Psalm 32:1-5
- Psalm 51:1-10
- Psalm 139:23-24
- Proverbs 28:13-14

Yielding: Does getting free have to be hard and scary?

Our beloved dog, Smudge, gave us a terrible scare when she was a puppy. One night, while I (Julie) was fixing dinner, I heard my son say, "Whatcha got, Smudge?" I stopped to see what was happening, but I couldn't see that she had anything in her mouth, so I went back to what I was doing. Suddenly Smudge started to thrash around, pawing at her snout and literally banging her head on the kitchen floor.

My first thought was, "Oh, God, how do you do the Heimlich maneuver on a puppy?" I picked up all six pounds of her and held her vertically, trying to get whatever was in her mouth to fall out. It didn't. She started thrashing around in my arms, so I put her on the floor. She started shaking and banging her head again frantically. When she stopped, I tried to open her mouth, but she wouldn't let me touch her head.

Just then, my husband walked in the door. "Steve, she's got something stuck in her mouth or throat, and she can't get it out." As if on cue, Smudge started thrashing and banging her head on the floor again. Steve took one look and responded decisively. We sped all the way to the vet, hazard lights flashing.

I held Smudge in my lap, and she continued to periodically thrash her head against my leg as we drove. We were too late. The vet had just gone home, and the assistant who was locking up would only direct us to a nearby emergency veterinary hospital. We drove off again, irritated and distraught. On the way, we saw another vet's office, so we drove in there, but they were closed, too. We sat for a moment in the parking lot, trying to figure out how to get to the veterinary hospital.

Smudge, by this time, was exhausted and breathing heavily. I worried that she was going into shock. She was in a cold sweat, and my clothes were covered in clumps of hair. (She is a breed that does not shed unless utterly stressed out.) I implored her in soft tones to let me help. This time she put up no resistance. I gently opened her mouth wide enough to expose the problem: Stuck tight to the roof of her mouth was a round felt pad, the kind that you stick to the bottom of a chair leg so it doesn't scratch the floor. She had been trying to shake free of it, but it wouldn't budge. Poor thing! We spoke to her in loving, soothing tones as I gently pried it off the roof of her mouth and removed it.

From my perspective, the solution to her problem was easy. But initially she didn't trust me or understand that I could do for her what she couldn't do for herself. If she'd been willing to let me help right away, we wouldn't have spent all that time and energy looking for a vet. All she really needed to do was relax and trust herself to me in the middle of her distress. But she wasn't willing to do that until she'd utterly exhausted herself.

What an object lesson! How often have I worn myself out trying to shake free of negative thoughts, feelings, or behaviors I felt stuck with? I have thrashed around and banged my head in vain—too tormented to let anyone near me. Too stubborn to relax into a process that I didn't fully understand. Too proud and ashamed to let anyone help. Why does it often take stress, exhaustion, and desperation to make us willing to relax and receive the help we need? How much sooner and with how much less effort could we get freedom and relief if we were quicker to trust the heart of the One holding us? More willing to let Him probe our places of pain and fear so that He can heal us? I'm so grateful that His love never fails and that He never gives up. He doesn't even mind when we shed all over Him. When we finally stop striving, settle into His lap and yield, freedom and rest can come with surprising ease. It doesn't have to be hard or scary.

PRACTICAL APPLICATION

As we finish this first module, we want to offer a few more practical suggestions.

First, we encourage you to keep a spiritual journal. If you like writing, then you're probably already keeping a journal the way you want. Great! Keep it up! Keeping a journal is a great way to record what you're learning, and it enables you to review what the Lord has shown you. You can look back on it and see how much He has done in your life! However, journaling can take different forms and have different purposes, so we want to be clear about what we mean. We aren't talking about keeping a "diary" or using a journal to write down a detailed history of the day's events and your reactions. It is easy to get bogged down or discouraged if you think journaling means you have to write like a novelist, journalist, therapist, or historian.

What we're talking about is using your spiritual journal as a tool. Writing in a journal is a way of externalizing what's in your head and heart. It helps to get thoughts and feelings out and onto the page where you can literally see them and allow the Lord to speak to you about them. All you really need to do is date the page and start writing the first thing that comes to mind. Write anything you're thinking or feeling. It doesn't have to be pretty, poetic, spelled correctly, or even in the form of complete sentences. However it comes out is okay. No one is going to read it, and you're not getting graded, you're getting free!

Here is an example, if you need it, of how you might start journaling:

> "Jesus, I don't know what I'm supposed to write. I don't even know what I'm feeling right now, please help me. I want to hear what you're saying to me, and I want the noise of my distracted mind and heart to be quiet so I can hear you. Maybe I'm a little scared, if I'm being honest. Writing can be tedious. I don't know what I'm scared of. Or why. I know in my head you're good and you love me but I'm such a mess. I want to be free. Help!!"

Second, if you don't already, begin reading the Bible every day. An easy way to start is to read a Psalm a day and/or a chapter in Proverbs. There are 31 chapters in Proverbs, so you could start with the one that matches the day's date. The wisdom of Proverbs and the encouragement of Psalms are great ways to nourish your spirit and soul with the truth.

Finally, if you are already journaling and/or reading scripture every day, another suggestion is to keep track of your spiritual journey in a creative way. For example, find a large jar or box to decorate. The idea is to consider where you are with the Lord and to cultivate thankfulness. If you are experiencing a tough season that makes thankfulness difficult, pray it through. We can always find something to be thankful for, even in the middle of trials. Write a few words expressing where you are and what you are thankful for. Date the note and put it into your decorated container. You could also write down scriptures that speak to your heart, words of encouragement, or brief testimonies of answered prayer. As needed, you can review where you've been and how the Lord has sustained you, and you'll be encouraged and blessed all over again!

Journaling, reading the Bible, and recording points of prayer and gratitude are essential practices for disciples of Jesus Christ. As such, they are a fitting way to end this first module on basic concepts. We encourage you to keep up one or more of these suggestions as we progress through the rest of this manual. When you look back later, you will be amazed at how far you have come!

INDEED

MODULE 2

TRULY FREE

If you abide in my word, you are truly my disciples, and you will know the truth, and the truth will set you free (John 8:31-32, ESV).

As we stated in the introduction, to be free INDEED is to be free in truth (truly free), to be free in terms of a legal deed (legally free), and free in terms of our actions or deeds (practically free). Here in Module 2, we unpack some of what it means to be truly free in Christ.

Identity Theft: Who are you going to believe?

It is estimated that as many as 15 million Americans are victims of identity theft each year.[8] This issue of modern life has the potential to ruin credit scores, create debt, and leave one bankrupt. Our adversary, the devil, is also a master of spiritual and psychological identity theft. Although we may not have had our identities literally stolen, most of us have struggled at one time or another with understanding who we are—perhaps even to the point of feeling bankrupt of any understanding of ourselves or our purpose. Literal identity theft can leave one feeling violated, distraught, empty, and scared. But no basement hacker has anything on the one hacking spiritual identities, leaving victims struggling to understand who they are at their very core. The valued currency our enemy is so ruthlessly after in our lives is purpose. He is viciously against our sanctification. He wants to get us to trade our intended purpose—an authentic, loving relationship with the one true God—for a counterfeit that looks and feels good but ultimately leads to death (Proverbs 14:12).

---

8 https://fortunly.com/statistics/identity-theft-statistics/

In *Small Brown Dog's Bad Remembering Day* (see Module 1), the small dog forgot who he was and looked to others for his identity. This children's book illustrates how easily we accept what others say about us, whether true or not. They may have developed ideas about who we are without any true understanding of our God-given identity and purpose. Their view is inevitably biased by their perspective and filtered through their own experiences. Other people can't necessarily see us for who we are, and they certainly are not qualified to define us. Only our creator, God, can tell us who we are and why we're here.

It is vital for us to resist letting the enemy steal our identity because a false or unstable identity is the mechanism he uses to thwart God's purpose for our lives. Purpose refers to the reason for which something exists or is done, made, used, etc. How can we discover and walk in purpose when we are stuck in cycles of questioning who we are? A nail will have a hard time discovering that its purpose is to hold things together if it thinks it's a hammer. Without a clear sense of identity, we are vulnerable to double-mindedness, doubt, depression, apathy, aimlessness, and lack of fulfillment. The human identity crisis began in the garden and is, at its root, caused by a lack of understanding of who God is. To be truly free, we need to believe the truth about God so that we can hear clearly what He says about us. Therefore, we need to unpack the subtle but commonly believed lie that God is not good.

Unpacking Lies: Is God truly good...to me?

Imagine a backpack stuffed so full of heavy items that it is hard to zip up. As you force it closed you wonder if the seams will hold. Now imagine carrying this heavy backpack 24/7. Exhausting! That's what it's like in our spirits when we carry a lifetime of painful memories, failed relationships, current stresses, overwhelming emotions, negative beliefs, and even physical pain. We need the Holy Spirit to help us unpack our bags and be rid of what weighs us down and slows our progress in the faith. He wants to help us sort through our baggage and let go of what we don't need. He wants us to dig deep and unpack the lies at the bottom of the bag.

Some of the most life-changing moments I (Sally) have ever experienced have come smack dab in the middle of a very ordinary day. Several years ago, I had such a moment while cooking dinner for my family. Standing at the stove, just stirring a pot, I felt a strong need to pray for a friend. Although I had not seen her in many years and did not know what triggered the feeling, I felt led to pray about areas of jealousy. As I did so, the Holy Spirit asked me if I understood the root of jealousy. I realized I had never really given it much thought, so He tutored me (John 14:26). I heard Him say that jealousy torments us when we believe the lie that God is good to others, but He is not fully good to me.

That day was the beginning of me learning to unpack the load I'd been carrying. As the Father identified an area of need, He would "unpack" it and show me what was underneath the unwanted action, thought, or feeling. He would help me see where I had believed the lie that He is not fully and truly good and the actions that grew around that lie to keep it in place. As a negative emotion would surface, rather than trying to fight it off, bury it, or deny it even existed, I would ask the Holy Spirit to "unpack it" for me, to show me the behaviors that had developed around the lie and where I had allowed it and agreed with it. Many, many things I had believed about myself and others were rooted in the subtle lie that God was not fully good or trustworthy.

This is nothing new or unique to me. Satan used the same strategy with Adam and Eve in the garden. He undermined their confidence in God and led them to eat the fruit of the knowledge of good and evil, plunging humanity into sin and misery. It worked then, and it still works today.

And the woman said to the serpent, "We may eat the fruit from the trees of the garden except the fruit from the tree which is in the middle of the garden. God has said, you shall not eat of it, neither shall you touch it, lest you die." But the serpent said to the woman, "you shall not surely die, For God knows that in that day you eat of it your eyes will be opened and you will be like God, knowing the difference between good and evil, blessings and calamity." And when the woman saw that the tree was good (suitable, pleasant) for food and that it was delightful to look at, and a tree to be desired in order to make one wise, she took of its fruit and ate and she gave some to her husband and he ate (Genesis 3:2-6, AMPC).

The word "satan" means slanderer and accuser. At the root, when you unpack original temptation, you see satan slandering the character of God. We believe the "root" of the fall was the false accusation that God is not trustworthy or completely good because He is withholding something good.

This lie had a partial truth in it. It's a common strategy of the enemy to take a small amount of truth and mix in a heaping helping of falsehood. Too often the bit of truth hooks us and we swallow the whole thing. Satan insinuated that God was not good because He was holding out on Adam and Eve, withholding something desirable. In truth God *was* holding something back. But it was **NOT** desirable! He was holding back the experiential knowledge of evil and calamity. These were things they could not have understood because they had never experienced anything remotely evil before! Adam and Eve lived in the perfection of God's original design and purpose for them. They had only known good and blessings. How could they have had any concept of evil and calamity? God's withholding was for their good.

When satan convinced Eve (and Adam) that God was unfairly withholding something, she unwittingly bought into the lie that God is not absolutely good. She and Adam gave into the temptation to know for themselves. They chose the fruit and the knowledge it gave them—knowledge of good and evil. Their choice was idolatry—putting themselves in God's place and trusting their own judgment over His. They failed to trust God's heart. They failed to believe that even if He was holding back something, He had a good, loving reason for doing so. They trusted in their own ability to handle the knowledge of good and evil more than they trusted God's heart and His wisdom.

This lie is at the root of many of our struggles. When something is messing with our thinking, tormenting us, or keeping us in spiritual, emotional, and behavioral bondage, we can learn to "unpack" the issue by asking the Lord to show us where we have believed the lie that He is not fully good. For example, when the Lord had me "unpack" jealousy, He showed me that underneath jealousy is the lie that God is good to others but not to me. Why? What is underneath that? The reason might be hidden feelings of shame, unworthiness, inferiority, or rejection stuffed beneath the jealousy.

I have received healing and freedom from envy and jealousy as I have allowed Father to deal with the issues of rejection and abandonment that were the deeper root problems. As He showed me how He saw me, I made the conscious decision to believe He is always good, even if my circumstances are not good. Even if I don't understand hard things I may be facing. Even when everything screams the opposite, God is still good and good to me. Long ago, I decided to make the Bible the foundational truth I stand on, regardless of what my feelings or circumstances may tell me. I do not see the beginning and the end, only He does. My understanding is limited, but His is not. Because He is good and true to His word, I can be assured that I am not rejected or abandoned. I am made worthy by the sacrifice of Jesus. Shame was dealt with on the cross. His word tells me that He made me and said that it was good! He loves me with an everlasting love. I love Him because He first loved me lavishly, wonderfully, and without reason. These promises are yours too:

I have loved you with an everlasting love; I have drawn you with unfailing kindness. I will build you up again, and you will be rebuilt (Jeremiah 31:3b-4a, NIV).

In this the love of God was made manifest (displayed) where we are concerned: in that God sent His Son, the only begotten or [unique [Son], into the world so that we might live through Him. In this is love: not that we loved God, but that He loved us and sent His Son to be the propitiation (the atoning sacrifice) for our sins (1 John 4:9-10, AMPC).

Having unpacked the lie that God is not good, we can take a fresh look at our identity and purpose. God gave humans dominion (rule) over the earth:

And God blessed them [granting them certain authority] and said to them, "Be fruitful, multiply, and fill the earth, and subjugate it [putting it under your power]; and rule over (dominate) the fish of the sea, the birds of the air, and every living thing that moves upon the earth" (Genesis 1:28, AMP).

Because they agreed with satan's lies, Adam and Eve lost their secure identities as innocent rulers of God's good world. The ground was cursed, and pain, heartache, toil, and death fell upon them and all creation (Genesis 3:14-21). Agreement with the accuser always leads to death and torment. This is why he still works hard to get us to question God's goodness and our identity in Christ. Even Jesus Himself faced this identity thief in Matthew 4:3. *If you are the Son of God, tell these stones to become bread.* IF. The enemy wanted Jesus to question His identity and act independently of God. But Jesus only ever did what He saw His Father do (John 5:19). He did not question His identity as a son of God, nor did He question His Father's goodness for one moment.

From the beginning, satan has been about stealing our identity as beloved sons and daughters of the Most High God. He gets us to question God's goodness in the world. "How could a loving God allow ...?" When we question his goodness to us, we are all too easily convinced by the lies the accuser tells us about ourselves and others. But Jesus came to redeem, to buy back, and to restore relationships. He never intended us to be separated from the love of God. That is not our natural state. We were created in His likeness to be in fellowship and to know Him. The cross means the restoration of all that was lost in the garden—our relationship with God, our identity and purpose, and our authority on the earth. Our righteousness (right standing) is in Christ, and He paid the price to give us right standing with the Father. You do not have to live in captivity anymore to sin, fear, addiction, or anything that is not a gift from the Father! *so that, as sin reigned in death, so also grace would reign through righteousness which brings eternal life through Jesus Christ our Lord* (Romans 5:21, AMP).

Whoever receives His testimony has set his seal [of approval] to this: God is true [and he knows that God cannot lie] (John 3:33, AMP).

As we discussed in Module 1, the enemy is a master at twisting perspective. He loves to make life appear like an Escher drawing where truth is hard to discern and confusion reigns, shifting our understanding of what is up or down. This is why the truth of God's word is so important. We need a plumb line or a compass that orients us to the true North of God.

God saw everything that He had made, and behold, it was very good and He validated it completely. And there was evening and there was morning, a sixth day (Genesis 1:31, AMP).

God is not a man, that He should lie, nor a son of man, that He should repent. Has He said, and will He not do it? Or has He spoken and will He not make it good and fulfill it? (Numbers 23:19, AMP).

These scriptures show us that God saw all that He made—including you and me—and declared it good. Our Father did not lie when He completely approved of His creation, and He will not change His mind. We are His kids, fully known and extravagantly loved! If we don't believe that, we are agreeing with the enemy instead of the word of God and what He says about us! Nothing we can do, say, or think can change the fact of His love for us. We all have pain from past experiences that scream at us that God is not good and we aren't either. Guilt and condemnation try to convince us that God could not possibly love us after what we have done. But when we repent, our sin is removed as far as the East is from the West. This is in no way a license to continue in sin; rather it is an invitation to more freedom!

PRACTICAL APPLICATION

Have you struggled to trust God and believe that He is good to you? Have you struggled to embrace your identity in Him as a beloved child? In the days ahead, the Lord will help you overcome unbelief and anything else at work to keep you in destructive, painful cycles. He will help you to "unpack" anything that keeps you from experiencing His goodness. The Father wants us to be free from torment, free to walk with Him in the garden of our hearts, and free to experience His presence without shame or fear. He drew you to Himself when you accepted His gift of salvation. If you believe His word is true, then allow it to be settled in your heart that He is good.

You may want to write on an index card, "God is absolutely good and good to me," and place it where you will see it every day. In addition (or instead), you can write out this paraphrase of Mark 9:24: "Lord, I choose to believe that You are absolutely good and good to me. Help me overcome any lingering unbelief."

Basic Needs: Is it okay to need more than just God?

We all need God. But is it true that God is all we need? Yes, but also no. No, because by God's own will and design, we do have legitimate biological and psychological "needs." These needs reflect our nature as bodily creatures who bear the image of the triune God. Thus, we are bodies in need of care and comfort. And we are hearts in need of connection, minds in need of understanding, and wills in need of autonomy (that is, the freedom to choose). Rather than denying these needs, we think it's healthier and more glorifying to God to recognize their legitimacy and allow Him to show us the best way to meet them.

Each of us begins life in a state of total dependence: We naturally receive the nurture and comfort we need. We trust that someone will supply all that is required for bodily life and emotional well-being. It is when that trust gets disappointed, when our need for nurture and comfort goes unmet, that difficulties begin. We will have more to say on this point shortly. For now, just note that although we grow out of infancy, we never really grow out of the need for comfort. It is part of our nature. And it is spiritually and psychologically healthier to recognize this need and learn to receive true comfort from God and others than to pretend it doesn't exist.

A second basic need is what psychologists call belonging or relatedness. It is the need for connection, the mutual giving as well as receiving of love, affection, and acceptance. The Trinity—God the Father, Jesus, and the Holy Spirit—live together in perfect trust and intimate harmony, and we are created in the image of this triune God. Thus, we are designed to relate to people in meaningful ways that anchor us in a shared reality. Without this connection we are vulnerable to mental illness. We will also waste energy looking for satisfaction from poor substitutes such as drugs, food, sex, fantasy, and media—all things that will never satisfy the real need. As the English clergyman and poet John Donne famously said, "no man is an island, entire of itself." We are social beings created to live in connection with others. If we cannot trust others because our first basic need for comfort and care went unfulfilled early in life, connection and intimacy will be hard later in life. But again, healing begins when we acknowledge the truth of our need for connection.

A third basic need is for understanding and competence (that is, the ability to live effectively). From infancy on, we work hard to understand our bodies, our relationships, our environment, and our place in the world. We are curious creatures, and we will go to great lengths to gain understanding and mastery.[9] As Solomon noted, *Wisdom is supreme; so acquire wisdom. And whatever you may acquire, gain understanding* (Proverbs 4:7). We don't all need to have degrees or other recognized "achievements," but we do all want to feel like we have a good understanding of reality and that we are effective in living our lives. We need understanding because, with wisdom, it leads to competence and mastery. With it we are equipped to function in the world and capable of pursuing goals.

Fourth, we were created with a need for autonomy, which is the need to have and exercise free will. Although Adam and Eve chose poorly from the get-go, God will never revoke the gift of free will (Romans 11:29); the need for autonomy and freedom is part of our design. God knew the risk He was taking in giving us personal control, but love isn't love if it's forced and not free. So, free will is essential to love, and it is essential to well-being. As we've discussed, the key to living happily in our freedom, the key that Adam and Eve threw away, is to believe that God is one-hundred percent good. With trust in His absolute goodness, we will want to make good choices that align with His desire and design for our lives. That is, we will exercise our free will with Godly wisdom. But if we go through life with a chip on our shoulders and the assumption that God is just trying to take away all our fun, then we will act out of rebellion and find it difficult to make good, righteous choices for ourselves. God has never been a control freak or a mean, stingy father; He gives us freedom because He loves us. True freedom is the ability to make good choices that are loving toward God, others, and ourselves (Mark 12:30-31).

---

9 We will even endure pain for the sake of gaining information, even when the information is useless! (https://www.science.org/content/article/humans-will-trade-pain-useless-information)

Finally, the balanced pursuit of these four needs leads to the greatest psychological well-being.[10] If we pursue the need for understanding, for example, over and above any other need, we may well be super-smart and accomplished, but we won't be as happy as if we were also pursuing other needs, such as meaningful relationships. So, the goal as we continue this journey toward greater freedom is to allow the Lord to show us areas where we are out of balance and how to pursue getting our needs for comfort, connection, understanding, and autonomy met in healthy ways. He knows our needs, and He will richly supply (Matthew 7:7-10; Philippians 4:19).

PRACTICAL APPLICATION

If you are struggling in any of these areas, we strongly recommend that you look up and read the following scriptures. God desires to meet all our needs, and he is more than able (Philippians 4:19)! For those verses that speak to your heart, consider writing them out in your journal or on an index card and memorizing them. The word of God is a weapon of warfare, a sword (Ephesians 6:17). It enables us to cut through the lies of the enemy and quickly come into agreement with what God says about us.

Comfort/Security
Psalm 23
Psalm 86
Isaiah 66:13
2 Corinthians 1:3-5
Matthew 5:4
Psalm 34:18
Psalm 91
Psalm 4:8
Psalm 12:5
Psalm 46:1
2 Thessalonians 3:3
Proverbs 18:10

Belonging/Acceptance
1 Corinthians 12
John 17:6-24
Ephesians 2:11-22
Romans 12:5
Genesis 2:18
Proverbs 18:1
Acts 2:42-47
Ecclesiastes 4:9-12
Hebrews 10:24-25
Proverbs 17:17
Ephesians 4:1-6
Psalm 133:1

---

10 Sheldon, K. M., & Niemiec, C. P. (2006). It's not just the amount that counts: Balanced need satisfaction also affects well-being. *Journal of Personality and Social Psychology, 91*(2), 331-341.

Competence	Autonomy/Choice
Psalm 119 (all, but esp. 65-72)	Deuteronomy 30:19-20
Proverbs 2:1-10	Joshua 24:15
John 16:13	Psalm 119:30
Exodus 35:31	Colossians 3:17
1 John 5:20	Ephesians 4:1
2 Timothy 2:15	Genesis 2:16-17
Job 12:12	Genesis 4:7
Proverbs 15:32	Isaiah 1:19-20
Isaiah 50:4	Proverbs 3:1-12
Luke 1:3-4	John 10:27
Luke 24:27	Romans 12:2
Acts 17:11	Romans 14:13-23

The Enemy Doesn't Play Fair: How can I know what I'm up against?

Our enemy, the devil, prowls about looking for and engineering opportunities to steal, kill, destroy, and devour (John 10:10; 1 Peter 5:8). The enemy doesn't play fair. When he sees you weak and vulnerable, he will attack without compassion or compunction. If he sees that you are young and knows that there is a call on your life (which is true of all of us, see Ephesians 2:10), he will go after you with a vengeance. He doesn't care if you're just a little child. For him, that's the best time to wreak his havoc and inflict his damage. If he can cripple you when you're young, then he scores a long-term victory. Most people are saved before they are eighteen, and most people experience their deepest wounds and traumas before they are eighteen.[11] Youth is a tremendous battleground between the spiritual forces of good and evil. Thankfully, the Lord never gives up on us, and He doesn't leave us as orphans. He wants to help us identify the lies we've believed about ourselves, about others, and about Him. When we also admit our need for Him, He can begin to work with our spirit, soul, and body to bring freedom.

I (Julie) want to share an example of how the Holy Spirit can reveal truth that will set us free, even after years of struggling in bondage to the enemy's lies. While getting some training on inner healing, I heard the story of a woman who grew up believing that people did not like her. She suffered for nearly 50 years under a rejection spirit. (We have more to say about this

---

11 https://home.snu.edu/~hculbert/ages.htm

in Module 3.) She experienced many hurts and rejections over the course of her life and suffered tremendous emotional torment. When she was in her 50s, she heard about a prayer ministry that might bring her relief and freedom, so she decided to schedule a session. What could it hurt?

In the session, the Holy Spirit identified for her the root of her torment. The seed of rejection had been planted when she was only three or four years old. She recalled the time when her extended family was together and the adults were talking in the living room. She had come in from outside and heard them talking, laughing, and enjoying themselves. When she walked into the room, everyone suddenly fell silent. They just looked at her and then looked awkwardly at each other. No one said a word. The little girl had no idea what was going on. Why did they suddenly stop talking and having a good time? She felt horrible. As the desire to cry welled up, she ran from the room feeling rejected and somehow ashamed.

She thought they had stopped talking because they didn't like her and didn't want her around. To make matters worse, she heard them begin talking again after she ran from the room. Feeling alone and vulnerable, the enemy lied to her and said, "See, they don't like you. No one wants you around. You're no fun." From that moment on, she believed that people didn't like her or want her around, and she unwittingly cooperated with and lived out this lie. The incident was forgotten, but its impact remained.

When she sought out prayer ministry as an adult, the Holy Spirit brought this memory to mind. Then He helped her remember, too, that the very next day, her family and extended family threw her a surprise birthday party! Would they do that for a child they didn't love or want around? Of course not. The truth was her family had all gone quiet when she entered the room because they had been discussing and planning her surprise party. They didn't want to spoil it! In those awkward, silent moments, no one knew what to say. Sadly, that uncertain, anxious moment was all the enemy needed to plant the seed of rejection that he tended and fertilized for decades. It took listening to and yielding to the Holy Spirit to identify the lie and replace it with the truth and to begin the process of getting free from the rejection she'd suffered with for so long.[12]

---

12 This process can take time because, as we noted in Module 1, we are spirit, soul, and body. Truth sets us free to begin the process of retraining habits of the mind and heart. But these new patterns require consistent time and effort to solidify.

As we outlined in the Introduction, the first step of the Free INDEED process is to invite the Holy Spirit to identify any area in our lives where we are stuck or enslaved. Where and in what ways do we need more freedom? With your spiritual journal open and dated, go ahead and ask the Holy Spirit about it. Write whatever comes to mind. As you read through the next section, allow Him to examine your heart, mind, and will to show you ways you may have built your life on a faulty foundation or responded as a wounded child. Allow Him to reveal areas of brokenness, pain, or trauma. Rest in the promise of His unfailing love. Ask Him if there are lies you have believed about Him. What He reveals He also wants to heal.

Childhood Social and Emotional Development: What is normal?

We present the following information on child development because we believe it is helpful for understanding both what is part of a normal developmental process and for understanding where, how, and why people get stuck. This information cannot take the place of asking the Lord to help you identify where you need freedom. At the same time, the understanding it provides may help you see things you've never considered. It may help you see yourself through the true lens of God's perspective (not a worm's or a bird's eye).

Many of our basic assumptions about ourselves and others come from childhood misperceptions, like the woman who mistook silence in the room for rejection. The self-protective strategies we develop often serve us well and help us cope for a season. This woman learned to protect her heart by rejecting others first before they could reject her. As another example, I (Julie) put on a tough-girl persona as a child to avoid further abuse after an unfortunate incident with a neighborhood boy. It worked for many years. No one dared to mess with me. But it also left me very lonely. As an adult, this defense mechanism is no longer necessary or effective. What once protected me now hurts me when it keeps me isolated and disconnected. As adults, whenever the Lord identifies an issue, we need Him to help us release the old hurts and habits and learn to walk in His ways.

When I was a child, I talked like a child, I thought like a child, I reasoned like a child. When I became a man, I set aside childish ways (1 Corinthians 13:11).

Truth trumps childish understandings. There comes a time when each of us must choose to set aside childish things and pursue the deeper things of God. To do so requires resolve and persistence. One-and-done prayers don't usually suffice because we are talking about habit patterns that have been long established in our nervous system. (We'll have more to say about the practical aspects of pursuing freedom in Module 4.) But getting more freedom requires that we first surrender outdated defense mechanisms and childish ways of talking, thinking, and reasoning. If we refuse, we will remain enslaved to the elementary principles of this world. Learning to adult is a good thing—even though it may sometimes seem like it's more fun and freer to stay childish. We are to walk in childlike faith and trust, but if we consistently choose not to grow up, it's like choosing to stay a slave. Put differently, the path of freedom is the path of maturity.

I mean that the heir, as long as he is a child, is no different from a slave, though he is the owner of everything, but he is under guardians and managers until the date set by his father. In the same way we also, when we were children, were enslaved to the elementary principles of the world. But when the fullness of time had come, God sent forth his Son, born of woman, born under the law, to redeem those who were under the law, so that we might receive adoption as sons. And because you are sons, God has sent the Spirit of his Son into our hearts, crying, "Abba! Father!" So you are no longer a slave, but a son, and if a son, then an heir through God (Galatians 4:1-7, ESV).

Prayer for Growth and Maturity

Abba Father, I want to grow up! I want to grow in both freedom and maturity. Show me what I need to see today and in the days ahead. Give me grace to grow one day at a time. I choose to trust You. I choose connection with You. I seek Your wisdom and understanding. I align my will with Yours today. All that I need is found in You. Guide me in Your truth and teach me; my hope is in You (Psalm 25:5). Amen.

Stages of Social and Emotional Development

When our mother, father, or other caregiver is attuned to our emotional and physical needs as infants, we feel comforted and settled and like we belong in the world. On this foundation of trust, we begin to build a sense of who we are, what we can and cannot do, and why we are here. We begin to take risks and make emotional connections with people outside our immediate family. We understand ourselves as social beings who need acceptance, worth, and a sense of purpose. We choose to pursue our interests and make our way in the world. At least, that is the ideal pattern. But if our needs for nurture, connection, understanding, and autonomy are inconsistently met or, worse, neglected, we will have a difficult time valuing ourselves or connecting with others (or God).

In my discipline of psychology, there are different theories about basic human needs, attachment, and the processes of social and emotional development. The nuances are beyond the scope of this book, so I (Julie) have chosen to summarize just one useful, descriptive framework.[13] According to this framework, we all encounter predictable social and emotional challenges at specific stages of development. How these challenges play out in our environment and how we resolve them sets the stage for development into the next stage. If a given challenge is resolved in a positive, healthy manner, we develop a predictable "virtue" or basic strength. But if the challenge is unresolved and a need thwarted, the negative outcome leaves a wound that undermines healthy development in later stages. For example, toddlers who have had their will broken rather than nurtured often struggle with shame, self-doubt, and self-control. Left unhealed, these wounds make it difficult to develop confidence, competence, and connection in later stages of growth.

Infancy: Trust vs. Mistrust

When infants cry, the caregiver's job is to discern and meet the need—for a diaper change, food, a nap, or cuddles. When tuned-in caregiving happens consistently and reliably, infants develop the "virtues" of trust, re-silience, and hope. Well-nurtured infants develop the ability to tolerate discomfort (e.g., hunger or a wet diaper) because they trust that someone

---

13 Erikson, E. H. (1950). *Childhood and society.* Norton.

Erikson, E. H., & Erikson, J. M. (1997). *The life cycle completed.* Norton.

cares and will surely provide for their comfort soon.

Unfortunately, not all infants are well-nurtured. What often happens is that caregiving is inconsistent or withheld, leading infants to lose hope and trust in others. Thus, abandonment, fear, anger, and despair can all take root in infancy. When caregiving is unpredictable, infants develop the mindset that no one is going to be there for them. This wounded trust typically leads to one of two reactions. The first is to develop an unhealthy level of self-sufficiency and independence. "If I don't take care of myself, no one else will." These children grow up to be fiercely independent, and they have a very difficult time trusting anyone. A second reaction is unhealthy dependence on others, as if to make up for what was not provided in infancy. In this case, the adult is anxious, needy, and "clingy" in relationships. Both response patterns reflect a basic lack of trust—a nervous system wired to interpret discomfort as an early warning sign that it's going to get worse if we don't do something now! If you see yourself in either pattern you may want to ask the Lord to restore basic trust, starting with your trust in Him. Feel free to use the following "Prayer to Restore Basic Trust," or write out your own prayer. Then we suggest you pray daily for restoration until you recognize and see that trust is growing and maturing within you.

Prayer to Restore Basic Trust

Lord, thank You for helping me see that my basic trust in You and in other people has been damaged. I need You, Father, to restore my ability to trust You and to trust other people. As an act of my will, I choose to disagree with the enemy of my soul who would tell me that it is safer to hold onto my mistrust and cynicism. I choose to disagree with the lie that isolation is preferable to connection. I ask You to forgive me for agreeing with the lie that You are not completely trustworthy. And I choose to forgive those people who have betrayed my trust. I name them now, and I release each one to Your righteous judgment, declaring they owe me nothing: _____. I acknowledge that my choice to forgive them does not mean that I suddenly trust them again. Trust is earned, and those individuals may never be worthy of my trust again. But I thank You, Father, that by forgiving them, I can be set free to trust You and others again in a new and deeper way. Thank You for setting me free, and I exalt You and Your truth over the enemy's lies. I declare my intention to grow in love and trust, with You by my side. In the name of Jesus Christ, Amen.

Toddlerhood: Autonomy vs. Shame/doubt

Toddlers are famous for phrases like "No!" and "I do it myself!" As we grow in self-understanding and self-awareness, we begin to push the boundaries of what we can do on our own. We want to explore and exercise our independence and do as much for ourselves as possible. We learn the power of the word "no," and we learn that exercising our will has palpable consequences! The positive outcome by the end of our toddler years is a healthy sense of independence and autonomy—the ability to do things for ourselves and to exercise free will.

These are the potty-training years, and they are challenging for caregivers. As children learn to eliminate properly, feed and dress themselves, etc., accidents, messes, and delays are inevitable. These things can be enormously frustrating for caregivers who want to live poop-free, mess-free, and delay-free! It takes wisdom and patience to provide appropriate boundaries and support so toddlers can develop self-regulation skills within a physically and emotionally safe context. Not all adults have such virtues. Conflicts and clashes of will happen, and often the need to keep the child safe and/or obedient trumps the need to explain patiently. As a result, children easily internalize shame, anger, fear, and other misperceptions. Because the child lacks language and vocabulary, the caregiver may not even realize they've hurt and confused the child. Even at this young age, the emotional brain is fully functional and has been since birth. We can feel fear, anger, sadness, delight, surprise, and disgust even though we lack the language to express our feelings and even though we cannot fully understand our circumstances. Our emotional brain (the limbic system) will react, but the rational brain (the frontal lobes) can't completely understand or explain what's happening. For instance, if you were yelled at or spanked when you crawled near the fireplace, you will have had an emotional reaction such as fear or anger. You may remember the incident, but because your brain was not fully developed, you won't have a tag on that emotional memory that reads, "Mom was just trying to protect me." All you will remember is the feeling of fear, anger, confusion, and/or frustration. These intense experiences can plant seeds of shame, self-hatred, or self-doubt in our nervous system.

We will have more to say about rejection, shame, and fear in Module 3. For now, it might be a good time to ask the Lord if some of your need for more freedom is rooted in this stage of development. Give Him permission to reveal and heal any lingering pain or trauma.

Preschool: Initiative vs. Guilt

The preschool years are characterized by explosive growth and learning as well as the desire to try new things. Initiative—the readiness to lead and make things happen on one's own—is an important skill that every child must learn. We need initiative throughout life for both simple things (like getting up in the morning) and for more consequential things (like deciding to apply for a job or starting a creative project).

The process of learning to take initiative, of course, is bound to lead to mistakes in judgment. For example, I (Julie) have a friend whose two preschool-aged children decided to "make Mommy happy" by painting her a rainbow. They were truly excited about their project and believed it would bring a big smile to her face. So, on their own initiative, they found paint and brushes and a canvas. When the project was complete, they excitedly brought Mommy to the playroom (she'd been doing dishes) to show her the rainbow. Her reaction wasn't quite as happy as they'd hoped, however, because the paint they had found was her expensive Italian oil paint and the "canvas" was the carpet. The rainbow arched from wall-to-wall on the playroom floor! Their intention and the initiative they showed was innocent, but the outcome was not at all good.

Can you think of a time when taking initiative as a small child led to a negative reaction from an adult? Do you remember feeling guilty or bad about yourself? Did you vow not to take initiative again? This kind of response to failed initiatives can lead to passivity and helplessness. We may conclude (usually implicitly rather than consciously) that nothing we do turns out right. Consequently, we abdicate the right to dream, plan, and initiate with joy and hope. Alternatively, we can have a rebellious reaction, refusing to feel any guilt at all. Either response is rooted in unresolved feelings of guilt and shame when our plans and initiatives didn't go well.

School Age: Industry vs. Inferiority

What psychologists mean by "industry" in this stage of social/emotional development is having a sense of competence in one or more areas. In elementary school, we begin to compare our knowledge, skills, and abilities to others. If we are not as good as someone else, we notice and feel bad. How we deal with that discomfort reveals a lot about our emotional and psychological health. In general, everyone needs to feel adequate to the task, whatever the task may be. Children who rarely feel adequate end up being emotionally and psychologically disabled, finding it difficult to relate to others socially or intimately without feeling personally threatened or easily put on the defensive. If you or someone you know is easily offended or threatened, it may be that negative experiences from this stage of childhood are part of the problem.

I (Julie) still remember how I felt when I saw a classmate's drawing in fifth grade. We were creating a poetry book, and everyone was required to draw a cover page. I was a good student and accustomed to doing very well on every assignment. When I saw Jeff's dinosaur drawing, I felt inferior by comparison. I could not draw like that, and I hated feeling inferior—especially in school. But rather than try to get better at drawing, I told myself I didn't like drawing. This response is typical when we fear being judged. I took my current (real) inferiority in the realm of drawing as evidence that I could never draw. I avoided art as much as possible after that.

I got away with that strategy because I was good at other things. I had competence ("industry") in other subjects, and I was good at music and sports. But those who are emotionally abused may not have anyone who believes in them or affirms their skills and competencies in any area. In such circumstances, it is difficult to navigate life without feeling threatened or becoming easily offended and defensive when someone tries to correct you about something. We all need a sense that we are effective and capable, and the stresses of life are harder to manage when we have a lingering sense of inferiority or when we question our preparedness to "do life."

When it comes to how we relate to God, if we hate being corrected or feel inadequate and unloved every time we need correcting, then we're going to have a hard time growing up and getting free. We will be slow to improve and change. Why? Because the need to improve and change confirms our worst fear—that we aren't good enough. The counterproductive logic at work here is that change and improvement appear to prove our current inferiority or inadequacy. We can't face feeling inadequate. It hurts too much and confirms to our hearts that the people (teacher, father, mother, sibling, classmate) who abused us were right all along. Rather than try to improve, we try to hide our need for improvement and even actively avoid opportunities to improve and grow up. It's a vicious cycle that gets us nowhere.

Adolescence and Beyond

Beginning sometime in middle school, children begin the life-changing experience known as puberty. These are turbulent years for all of us as we become strangers and aliens to our own bodies. We begin to self-consciously seek answers to questions like "Who am I?" "Why am I here" "What should I be doing?" With a solid foundation of trust, confidence, and hope—developed in the context of loving relationships—we are positioned to find satisfying answers to these questions. With or without belief in God, many psychologically well-adjusted individuals advance through adolescence and adulthood with a stable sense of self, with integrity and purpose. They find personally satisfying answers to these questions and live a productive and fulfilling life, body and soul.

As Christians, however, we know that we are body, soul, and spirit, and no answer to the question "who am I" is truly complete apart from God. We, too, must wrestle with our identity and calling. But when we are "stuck" in an earlier stage of social and emotional development—when we cannot fully trust God or other people, when we doubt our ability to make good decisions or feel guilty about our choices, when we feel worthless and inferior to most everyone else—then we cannot be fully alive and receptive to what God says about who we are. Of course, what He says about us is that we are loved. We are accepted. We are forgiven. We are chosen. We are adopted into God's family, and we have a place at the table. We have a purpose and a job to do in the family business. (See Ephesians chapter one.) These things are true. The real question is, can you receive these truths for yourself? Can you freely ask God for more and seek Him for the specifics of your identity and calling? If you are stuck or emotionally shut down, doing so will be hard.

May we all continue to grow in maturity and freedom and get healed of past hurts so that we can move on and live the abundant life to which we have been called in Christ Jesus.

Aversive Childhood Experiences: Do they matter?

Childhood and adolescence matter for adult functioning—for how we treat ourselves and how we relate to God and others. But as we've seen, growing up is hard to do. The heartbreaking truth is that safe, stable, loving families are the exception, not the rule. A landmark study in the mid-1990s, involving over 17,000 adults, examined how childhood experiences of abuse and neglect affect physical health and well-being in adulthood.[14] Among the study's major findings were that two-thirds of the adult participants reported at least one aversive childhood experience such as emotional abuse, physical abuse, sexual abuse, physical neglect, emotional neglect, family violence, family substance abuse, divorce, mental illness, or a family member's incarceration. One in five people (20%) reported experiencing three or more of these things.

The study also found that aversive childhood experiences (ACEs) strongly predicted poor health and well-being throughout life. As the number of ACEs increases so does the risk for the following:

• Poor academic achievement
• Poor work performance
• Financial stress
• Suicide attempts
• Early initiation of smoking
• Early initiation of sexual activity
• Adolescent pregnancy
• Multiple sexual partners
• Risk for sexual violence
• Sexually transmitted diseases
• Alcoholism and alcohol abuse
• Liver disease
• Chronic obstructive pulmonary disease
• Ischemic heart disease
• Illicit drug use
• Depression
• Health-related poor quality of life

Aversive childhood experiences also affect brain development. Violence, abuse, and conflict in the home can actually hardwire the nervous system to be hypervigilant, meaning to be easily triggered into "fight or flight" mode.[15] Sometimes children respond to severe trauma by spacing out—literally tuning out reality. In this case, the brain goes "off-line." Both response patterns, hypervigilance and shut down, can carry into adult ways of dealing with problems and upsets. Our nervous system adapts to our early environment which sets the stage for how we react to events and situations later in life.

14 https://www.cdc.gov/violenceprevention/aces/
15 Graham, A. M., Fisher, P. A., & Pfeifer, J. H. (2013). What sleeping babies hear: A functional MRI study of interparental conflict and infants' emotion processing. *Psychological Science, 24*(5), 782-789.

Knowing the truth of our basic human needs for nurture, connection, understanding, and the exercise of free will (what psychologists call autonomy and what God calls freedom), knowing about the normal stages of social/ emotional development, and being aware of the common consequences of aversive childhood experiences can all be helpful in facing up to those areas in our lives where we are not free. No one can escape the human condition: we need others, and those we need and love will inevitably let us down at times. The deeper our disappointment, the deeper the wound. But if we can learn to sit still in our discomfort without denying it or excusing it, then we will be able to work through it and claim our freedom in Christ to love and be loved, to make free choices that are positive and productive rather than harmful and destructive, and to find our identity and purpose in Christ.

PRACTICAL APPLICATION

If you felt agitated, distracted, or uncomfortable while reading and thinking about basic needs and child development, these are useful clues. It is likely that the less you want to think about these things, the more you may need to ask the Holy Spirit to identify the specifics of what He wants to heal. It is difficult to stay still in our discomfort, but that is exactly the place where we need Jesus the most. He is sufficient to save, heal, and deliver us from the wounds we've received from others and the wounds we've inflicted on ourselves. We recommend memorizing and meditating on the following scripture as you allow the Lord to work in your life:

But I have calmed and quieted my soul [my emotions, my mind, and my will], like a weaned child with its mother; like a weaned child is my soul within me (Psalm 131:2, ESV).

_____

The "Shelf of I Don't Know": What do I do with unanswered questions?

As a former atheist who was not raised in church, I (Sally) didn't know the first thing about the Bible when I accepted Jesus at 28 years old. I dove in with a voracious appetite to learn. As a child, I was taught to be inquisitive and to find answers by studying for myself. In the early days of my faith, some of the things I read in the Old Testament were hard for me to get my head around. Why would God do some of this stuff? I have seen people struggle in their faith as their minds have been assaulted with doubts about God's love, truth, and goodness. The enemy loves to sow uncertainty, accusing God of unfairness, inconsistency, genocide, etc. If God is truly love, what's it all about?

I am not one to follow anything blindly, and I absolutely hate having unanswered questions. But I have found that just because I do not understand something right now does not mean that I won't grow in understanding. I decided long ago that I believe the word of God to be accurate. I have studied evidence for the validity of scripture, and I accept it.[16] Because His word is accurate and I believe it, I also believe that God is good regardless of my circumstances. Based on these convictions, I chose not to allow my questions to chip away at my faith. If I come across something in the Bible that I do not have clarity on, I shelve it. I literally picture in my mind a shelf where I place concepts that I don't yet fully understand, and I trust God to help me to understand them in His time. I call this my "Shelf of I Don't Know."

Over the years, shelving my questions (rather than ignoring them, denying them, wrongly judging, or answering them with shallow answers) has helped me stay settled in my faith even as I grow. It has prevented doubt and unbelief from getting a foothold. Over the years, many things have gone up on that shelf, and many things have come off as the Lord has shown me answers. The enemy would love for me to obsess over my questions and get me sidetracked or derailed in my faith. But by using the "Shelf of I Don't Know" (or the "Shelf of I Don't Know YET"), I avoid giving the enemy a foothold. My "shelf" is a way of choosing to trust that God is good. With it, I affirm that He loves me extravagantly and that I am lovesick for Him. He is worthy of my trust even when I don't fully understand His ways or "whys."

---

16 If you struggle with believing the Bible is valid and reliable, we encourage you to do some research. Discover for yourself what makes the Bible unique and valid compared to any other known manuscript. We provide a few classic references for further reading in the Apologetics section of our suggestions for further reading.

What are your unanswered questions? You may want to start your own "Shelf of I Don't Know Yet." Using your spiritual journal, date it and begin writing out as many questions as you can think of right now. You can always add to the list later. Father God cares about your questions, anxieties, doubts, and concerns. He is not threatened by them, and He doesn't disapprove of them. One by one He will settle you. You can trust Him to guide you and lead you into all truth (Psalm 25:5; John 14:26).

The Father's Heart: What if I don't feel God's love?

God's love is a fundamental aspect of the truth that sets us free. He is everything good, loving, noble, excellent, and praiseworthy. He is light, and in Him there is no darkness. We never need to feel the shadow of His back turning away from us in disgust, impatience, or disapproval. These are the truths that can set us free and set our hearts on fire in response! As cliche as it may seem, nothing can compare to the power of God's love. The Father wants us to know and experience how wide, how long, how high, and how deep His love for us truly is (Ephesians 3:18). He knows that the more we abide in His love, immersed and at peace, the freer we become.

So, what if we're not feeling it? What if we are numb and unresponsive? Can we really be free if we're frozen? Yes and no. Yes, because truth is independent of our feelings; our freedom in Christ, our status as positionally sanctified by the finished work of Christ, is true whether we feel it or not. So yes, you can be free in Christ while numb to His love and goodness. But also no. You are not truly experiencing freedom and love if you never experience the warmth of His freedom and love! Imagine refusing to walk after a break-through medical procedure to repair your spine. The surgeon declares you free and able to walk, but you refuse. You are too afraid to try. You know in your mind you are free to walk, you believe you can walk, and your heart's desire is to walk. But if you never actually walk, are you free to walk?

I (Julie) certainly wasn't. A turning point in my journey toward truly experiencing the Father's love happened in a counseling session. My counselor asked me to go to a favorite place in my mind where I felt safe and most like myself. For reasons I won't go into, I went to Dunnottar Castle, a Scottish coastal ruin that I had visited multiple times in my early twenties. In my mind, I saw Jesus and His mother, Mary, in a field outside the castle grounds. Mary represented a safe, trustworthy woman. She led me across the field and up to the castle wall. Jesus was now standing just outside the castle grounds, and I briefly exchanged eye contact with Him. But only Mary and I went into the castle ruins. (Honestly, at that time in my life, it was like me to keep Jesus nearby, but just outside my walls.) Mary took me to a high vantage point—a place on the castle wall overlooking the North Sea. As we gazed at the expanse, she put a nurturing arm around my shoulder, gestured across the sea, and said, "This is how much the Father loves you."

It was a breakthrough moment that gave me a meaningful picture of just how much the Father loves me personally. I wish I could say that everything changed dramatically after that moment, but that wouldn't be entirely accurate. Something changed, for sure. Any encounter with God's love will change a person. But I still had a heavy suitcase to unpack. Or, to use the analogy of a patient receiving a breakthrough surgery, I still needed rehab before being able and willing to walk.

Some years later, the scene on the North Sea changed during another unexpected encounter. This one occurred during corporate worship. The Lord brought to mind the scene I just described. But now Jesus was swimming in the water and inviting me to jump off the wall and swim with Him. By this time, I was mostly free of my heavy backpack, and I jumped! I *felt* the love of God. I experienced deep communion and connection to His heart.

PRACTICAL APPLICATION

None of us has experienced the Father's love to its full measure because its depth, width, breadth, and timeless length are more than we can comprehend. There is always more in God than we have yet grasped. All of us can benefit from a simple prayer for more of God. If you feel blocked in your ability to connect to God's love, we encourage you to ask Him about it. With your spiritual journal at hand, ask what's blocking the experience of His love. Be willing to write out any thoughts that come. Perhaps you still don't fully believe God is good to you. Or perhaps you still have some places of pain or bitterness that need healing and cleansing. Whatever it is, ask and you'll receive grace and mercy to unpack and discard whatever keeps you from experiencing God's love.

You can also choose to enrich your experience of God's love through worship music. Many, many songs and hymns have been written about the love of God. God is love, and we love Him because He first loved us. Romans 5:5 says He has poured out love into our hearts through the Holy Spirit. Worship is a way to respond to His love with gratitude and to deepen our connection with Him. We encourage you to find the worship songs that move your heart in worship, love, and gratitude and play them often.

Combating Double-mindedness: Why is it important to be settled?

Dear brothers, is your life full of difficulties and temptations? Then be happy, for when the way is rough, your patience has a chance to grow. So let it grow, and don't try to squirm out of your problems. For when your patience is finally in full bloom, then you will be ready for anything, strong in character, full and complete.

If you want to know what God wants you to do, ask him, and he will gladly tell you, for he is always ready to give a bountiful supply of wisdom to all who ask him; he will not resent it. But when you ask him, be sure that you really expect him to tell you, for a doubtful mind will be as unsettled as a wave of the sea that is driven and tossed by the wind; and every decision you then make will be uncertain, as you turn first this way and then that. If you don't ask with faith, don't expect the Lord to give you any solid answer (James 1:2-8, TLB).

It is not a natural human tendency to be happy when things are rough, but the word shows us that difficult seasons and situations help refine us. They help us grow in strength and character. Trials can cause us to draw close to God's heart if our hearts are seeking His. But if we're not careful, they can also cause us to accuse God and walk in doubt and unbelief when our prayers are not answered how we want them to be.

These verses in James show us that trials can bring growth when we let them and when we are seeking His heart. They also tell us that God is ready, willing, and able to give us the wisdom we need for every circumstance when we ask, believing He will answer. However, when we ask without faith we ask with double-mindedness. When our minds are wavering between two opinions (as Elijah put it in 1 King 18:21), believing God one moment and doubting Him the next, we are in for a ton of issues. We all have moments when our faith falters. The important question is, what do you do when that happens? When we run to the Father and pour out our hearts honestly, doubt and all, He will help us overcome our doubt and grow in faith (Luke 17:5). So, the problem comes when we choose not to deal with our lack of faith and simply allow double-mindedness to remain. It will make you unstable. Double-mindedness is like the shopping cart with the wonky wheel that makes it wobbly and difficult to steer in the right direction. We struggle unnecessarily in our walk with the Lord when we waiver like a wonky wheel on whether God is good, whether His promises are true, or whether He even really loves us.

Worry is another manifestation of double-mindedness. We may truly love God and want to follow Him. But when we worry, we entertain anxious what-if scenarios in our minds. To unpack it, worry boils down to fear and unbelief. Scripture tells us perfect love casts out fear (1 John 4:18). When we worry, we are not walking in perfect love. Worry makes us waiver between two opinions, flipping back and forth between believing God loves and cares for us, and feeling doubt and uncertainty about whether He's paying enough attention to keep us from harm.

Scripture says, *You will keep in perfect peace all who trust in you, all whose thoughts are fixed on you!* (Isaiah 26:3, NLT). We can have peace when our thoughts are not flipping back and forth between belief and doubt. Peace comes when our thoughts are settled on Him! To be clear, it really isn't a question of our love for Him. It's more about choosing to trust and choosing to throw off any thoughts that come against the goodness of God!

The passage from James is foundational as we grow and mature in our walk with God. Trials are not a slap on the wrist, the result of a lack of faith, or evidence that you are not in His favor. If these things were true, then Jesus' disciples would have been a sorry bunch indeed. They faced many trials and made many mistakes, but they matured and grew in their love for Jesus because they were all in, mind, heart, and will!

James also shows us how important it is to ask for wisdom and expect to receive it. When we allow ourselves to waiver and become double-minded, we will be unstable. An unstable mind is the shaky foundation on which many mental illnesses are built. It brings depression, anxiety, and any number of other maladies as one flips from faith in God's goodness to fear.

Combating double-mindedness starts with a decision to agree with the truth. Like the old hymn "I have decided to follow Jesus, no turning back, no turning back," we can make the decision to believe and not doubt. We choose to settle our hearts on the truth of His word. When hell comes against our minds, we throw those thoughts out and choose not to agree with them! When fear and doubt come in like an overwhelming flood, we seek His face and cry for help! You may still feel like there are barriers to being truly settled in the following declarations. You may struggle with issues, the pain and confusion of old wounds, wrong mindsets, or ungodly beliefs. But these struggles are separate from your choice to align with the truth and pursue healing no matter the cost.

We encourage you to keep choosing faith over fear and doubt. Decide that you want to be settled in Him. Choose to affirm your commitment to the truth. By making the following declarations—often and out loud—you affirm your choice to believe God and have a settled heart, no matter your circumstances or struggles.

- It is settled in my heart that God is good (Psalm 34:8, Psalm 100:5, John 3:16-17).
- It is settled in my heart that God loves me extravagantly (John 15:13, Romans 8:38-39, Song of Solomon 7:10).
- It is settled in my heart that God will never leave me nor forsake me (Deuteronomy 31:6, Psalm 94:14).
- It is settled in my heart that God is who He says He is (Isaiah 43:11-13, Isaiah 46:9, Revelation 1:8).
- It is settled in my heart that God is true to His promises (Romans 4:21, 2 Corinthians 1:20).
- I will not allow disappointment or unanswered questions to shipwreck my faith.
- I choose to love and believe God no matter what.

Gut Check: Do you want to be well?

The theme of this module is truth. If Jesus sets us free we are truly free. We have affirmed the foundational truth that God is good. We have taken an honest look at our human needs and the challenges that arise as we grow from infancy to adulthood. We have examined the need to apply our mind, heart, and will to pursue truth even through the struggles of unanswered questions, numbed emotions, and the temptation to doubt and be double-minded. Now we take a moment to do a gut check. Do you truly want to be well ... whole ... completely free?

Now there is in Jerusalem near the Sheep Gate a pool with five covered colonnades, which in Hebrew is called Bethesda. On these walkways lay a great number of the sick, the blind, the lame, and the paralyzed.[17] One man there had been an invalid for thirty-eight years. When Jesus saw him lying there and realized that he had spent a long time in this condition, He asked him, "Do you want to get well?" "Sir," the invalid replied, "I have no one to help me into the pool when the water is stirred. While I am on my way, someone else goes in before me." Then Jesus told him, "Get up, pick up your mat, and walk." Immediately the man was made well, and he picked up his mat and began to walk. Now this happened on the Sabbath day, so the Jews said to the man who had been healed, "This is the Sabbath! It is unlawful for you to carry your mat." But he answered, "The man who made me well told me, 'Pick up your mat and walk.'" "Who is this man who told you to pick it up and walk?" they asked. But the man who was healed did not know who it was, for Jesus had slipped away while the crowd was there. Afterward, Jesus found the man at the temple and said to him, "See, you have been made well. Stop sinning, or something worse may happen to you." And the man went away and told the Jews that it was Jesus who had made him well. Now because Jesus was doing these things on the Sabbath, the Jews began to persecute Him. But Jesus answered them, "To this very day My Father is at His work, and I too am working" (John 5:2-17).

When our basic needs go consistently unmet, we may lose hope over time, and that makes us heart sick (Proverbs 13:12). The man in this parable sat for 38 years waiting for healing. Year after year he watched others get their healing before he did, and his heart slowly hardened to the point that he couldn't even respond to Jesus' full offer. You see, Jesus asked him if he wanted to get well, meaning free from or recovered from infirmity or disease; completely cured; in good standing or favor, fortunate; being a cause for thankfulness, to an extent approaching completeness. Jesus was offering

---

17 Some, but not all, ancient manuscripts include: *awaiting the moving of the waters. For from time to time an angel descended into the pool and stirred the water. As soon as it was stirred, the first to enter the pool would be healed of his disease.*

him wholeness, but through his wounded perspective he couldn't see it. The text suggests that the man could have received physical healing had someone just brought him into the water when it was stirred. But Jesus didn't just put him in the stirred water because He was offering more than just physical healing. Jesus wanted this man to understand that His love was big enough to heal all the pain of years of loneliness, isolation, and unmet needs.

Jesus offered complete healing, salvation, and deliverance, but the man's capacity to receive it was atrophied. He got partial healing—in his body. But his actions show that he remained an emotional and spiritual invalid. His woundedness kept him from perceiving Jesus' real question: "Do you want to be well; do you want to be complete; do you want to be in good standing, forgiven; do you want a cause for complete thankfulness?" His response to Jesus was to dodge the question, complain, and shift blame. Jesus ignored this self-focused whining and told him simply to take up his bed and walk. He did that, but then he walked away without even saying thanks or bothering to find out his healer's name! Then, just as soon as the Jews called him out for carrying his bed on the Sabbath, he blamed the one who healed him! Later, he encounters Jesus again and learns his name. At this point, Jesus admonishes him to go and sin no more so that nothing worse happens. Defensively, he responds by going back to the Jews to tell them Jesus was the guy who had healed him and told him to carry his bed on the Sabbath. He is essentially throwing Jesus under the bus!

What is up with this guy? He was miraculously healed after 38 years of physical infirmity, but he needed much more emotional, relational, and spiritual healing. He doesn't get it, though, because he apparently didn't know he needed it. Time for a gut check. True freedom is found only in Jesus. We all need Him desperately, more than we can fathom. If the Son, Jesus Christ, sets us free we are truly free. This freedom is our birthright as sons and daughters of God. Do we want to be well? Do we want it more than anything? Are we willing to let go of pride and appearing to have it all together to run to Jesus like a child? Do we consider everything else as rubbish compared to Him (Philippians 3:8)? Are we grateful for His grace and mercy? When we say yes to Jesus, He promises to make us new.

This parable also shows us that Jesus' miraculous physical healing was actually an invitation into the more complete healing He had in mind. It was an invitation to take another step toward wellness and wholeness. The physical healing was like an appetizer meant to whet the palate. Or, to use a different analogy, the need for healing—this man's and ours—is like an onion. We all have layers and layers of misperceptions and misunderstandings—lies we have believed about ourselves and about God. On top of that are layers of bad choices and bad habits. We take encouragement from the fact that Jesus healed this man even after 38 years! But we don't want to ignore the gut check, the warning in this story that we need to be grateful and willing to recognize healing as an invitation to go on a journey with the healer. There is always so much more!

Therefore if anyone is in Christ, he is a new creation. The old has passed away. Behold, the new has come (2 Corinthians 5:17)!

To be a new creation in Christ is both a done deal and a continuing event in the same way that sanctification is both positional (done) and progressive (continuing). To be a new creation means to be founded and formed from nothing and with no input of one's own. There is no artwork, no building, no book, no cake or gourmet dinner that made itself. As God's new creation in Christ, there is absolutely nothing that you did or could ever do to help make this new you. Because of Christ alone we are new creations, literally meaning "fresh, novel, unprecedented." You are unprecedented and new in Christ today! And you will be new in Him again tomorrow! The work of coming into being as a new creation is a completed act of Christ with continuing effects, day after day after day!

There is tremendous freedom in knowing that we can count on Christ's finished work to continually make us new every morning and that there is nothing we can do to make that finished work more complete, more effective, or better looking! We are His continually new creation, and He doesn't need our help! We can resist Him, though, and slow down our progress. We can stunt our own growth, even refuse healing like the man at the pool, if we stubbornly refuse to trust His will over our own and refuse to give Him access to our hearts. But the life Jesus offers involves movement and growth. The nature of God's kingdom is dynamic; there is always more (Isaiah 9:7, Romans 11:33). Our part is to accept His invitation. To answer "yes, I want to be well and more well." To open our hearts and let Him do what needs to be done.

Prayer of Declaration

God, I declare my agreement with Psalm 119:68 that You are good and You do good! I give You my unanswered questions. I give You my heart, with all its pain, sorrow, and regret. I want to be well. I choose faith over fear. I believe You. Help my unbelief! I declare with 2 Corinthians 5:17 that today I am a new creation in Christ. My old self has passed away. I am free and alive in Christ. I am a fresh, novel, and unprecedented creation today and every day because of Your finished work on the cross! In Christ I will continue to become new day by day! I am truly free already, and I am getting freer day by day! In the name of Jesus Christ, Amen!

MODULE 3

LEGALLY FREE

So if the Son sets you free, you will be free indeed (John **8**:36).

Just as being born to your parents is enough to establish your identity as a son or daughter, so your belief in Jesus Christ establishes your identity as a child of God (John 3:3-16). As His children, we have positional freedom in Christ. We are truly free because Jesus Christ secured our freedom from sin and death through His undeserved death on the cross and His glorious resurrection from the dead! But like children, we must learn to walk in the fullness of our freedom. Progressive freedom and sanctification are about working out in body and soul what is already true in spirit.

Our focus in this module is on the ways we inadvertently give satan the legal right to harass us even after we have been born again. Excellent resources are already available on many of the topics we will address (see For Further Reading). Our goal is not to duplicate these resources but to offer a fresh perspective, to share what we have learned, and to provide practical suggestions and guidance.

Eviction Notice: Do I have to put up with this?

As I (Sally) have already mentioned, I identified as an atheist before Jesus drew me to salvation. I was physically healed at salvation, and from there God began a process of spiritual and emotional healing. Although God was at work in my heart in powerful ways, I was stumped as to why I wasn't free from all my junk immediately upon salvation. I hadn't yet learned about sanctification, much less the difference between positional, experiential, and ultimate sanctification. Before I understood the theology behind it, the Lord gave me an analogy that brought practical clarity and helped to settle my spirit, even when the process was slower than I wanted.

Imagine the purchase of an apartment building full of tenants. The buyer may hold a physical DEED to the building, but that does not mean the property is empty, clean, or perfect. It may well need renovation and repair. Typically, tenants are notified of a change in ownership along with any major renovations being planned. Some may decide to leave, but some will not. Unwelcome tenants who violate the lease agreement may be served an eviction notice. Even then, some will not willingly leave. These now unwelcome squatters may require a sheriff's deputy to come and personally escort them from the premises.

This analogy illustrates aspects of progressive sanctification, the process of walking out our freedom in Christ. At salvation, we signed over the legal deed to our lives. The purchase price for our freedom and abundant life (both now and for eternity) was the blood of Jesus. He now legally owns the deed to our lives. But there can be "tenants/squatters" from our past that live in our minds, hearts, and nervous systems. Some of these "tenants" leave simply because of the change of ownership, but some do not. Some leave as the "renovation" begins, and it is no longer comfortable—it no longer feels like home. Some will leave with an "eviction" notice of prayer. But some stubbornly remain. They need "deputies" to come help escort them out. That is, sometimes we need others (friends, pastors, prayer counselors, professional clinicians) to stand with us in prayer and wise counsel to enforce our legal freedom.

One thing that emboldens these "squatters" to stay is that in the past they were welcome and even valued tenants. For example, we may have welcomed and valued the spirit of anger because it gave us a sense of safety from further hurt or made us feel justified. More generally, when we carry unresolved pain or trauma, the enemy gets us inadvertently agreeing with ungodly and destructive thought patterns that seem to have some sort of "benefit."[18] For instance, no one wants to be an addict, but the spirit of addiction can take up residence when the "benefit" it brings gets us to open the door and allow it in. Being high helps one temporarily forget the pain of trauma, abandonment, rejection, shame, childhood abuse, etc. As fleeting as that reprieve may be, if we have no true resolution of the tormenting pain (that is, without healing/deliverance), we will want to feel better somehow,

---

18 We learned this concept from Brother Mike from the Arizona Deliverance Center. It brought great clarity to our freedom walk.

even for just a moment. The "benefit" can be a trauma-induced way to cope. The spirit of addiction works to compel us to use again and again and again.

Eventually, the "benefit" gets overshadowed by an overwhelming and controlling need to use, even though the "benefit" has long since expired. The person may genuinely want to quit, but by now, the tenant (the evil spirit of addiction) won't leave because it feels it has a legal right to stay. It's as though every choice to use provided an extension on the contract. It won't leave because it has a right to stay. So, it makes itself at home and partners with other lying spirits (e.g., self-sufficiency, isolation, etc.) that promise to help us cope with the pain. The enemy's camp works together well, creating a synchronized and strategically planned long game. Shame, guilt, and condemnation form a partnership to strengthen addiction and keep the cycle stuck on repeat. The torment increases as addiction works to destroy everyone and everything in its path. Remember, the thief comes to steal, kill, and destroy (John 10:10). We often do not take this scripture as literal, but it is. The enemy's end game is to take us out, and he will do it however possible. He may incapacitate us through wrong beliefs about ourselves or others that paralyze and torment us. Or he may capitalize on our unresolved trauma to literally kill us by creating suicidal ideation or prompting self-destructive/risk-taking behaviors.

The good news is that when we give Jesus the deed to our property (body, soul, and spirit), He gets to work on renovations! He has the authority to evict the squatters, but we must agree with Him that they need to go. Proverbs 26:2 tells us that a causeless, undeserved curse does not land. Through the finished work of Christ on the cross, He has removed the curse of sin and death and declared us blameless and righteous. We are no longer under a curse, and we do not "deserve" curses. Why, then, does it sometimes feel like we are cursed to repeat the same mistakes over and over? Paul articulates this struggle in Romans 7. Reading that chapter you may wonder, is freedom even possible? Yes! Can we evict the squatters, clean the place up, renovate, and change the locks? Yes! We do *not* have to put up with this! God is for us, and because of this we are more than conquerors (Romans 8)!

Nevertheless, we don't always walk in victory because sometimes we give curses cause to land through our beliefs, mindsets, behaviors, habits, and continuing agreement with the enemy. The enemy is a legalist. If we give him a "legal" inch, he'll take a mile. One of the greatest challenges we face in evicting "squatters" is that we become very attached to the "benefits." We like them; they serve us in our brokenness. And as long as we continue to like the benefit, we leave the door unlocked (or wide open). We need to pray for the grace to love what God loves and hate what He hates. God hates torment. We, too, must hate it enough to want to do something about it! God is already committed to our freedom. Our skin in the game is choosing to side with God about our freedom and being committed to walking it out.

"Benefits:" Are they worth more than freedom?

Walking it out can be challenging, especially when the old way of thinking and relating to people is more comfortable and even "comforting" to our pride or sense of self. For example, I stood at the sink one evening rinsing dishes and loading them into the dishwasher. My mind wandered and I found myself struggling with critical thoughts toward an individual who had treated me in an unloving manner. Although I had forgiven them for the incident, thoughts of my innocence and their guilt assaulted my mind. I was tempted to agree with thoughts that emphasized how I was the innocent victim who had been SO wronged. As my emotions joined in to strengthen the temptation, Father reminded me that I had forgiven the person and been set free. I was not to resurrect the pain or open the door to unforgiveness. He showed me how easy it is to LIKE the thinking that promotes the innocence of self and demonizes others without consideration of any part I may have played in the incident. Self-righteousness is a sleazy lawyer defending you in the court of your own self-justification. The Father showed me how this "lawyer" had me easily accepting the "benefit" he promoted—my self-righteousness at the expense of freedom. The "benefit" told me that I was right. I was justified in my victimhood! My mind struggled to fight off the desire to fill my heart with a smug feeling of superiority, a Pharisaical pride that I was better than the one who slighted me. UGH!!!!

But God reminded me of the forgiveness I had already decided on and revealed the enemy's tactic to deceive my mind by offering a "benefit" that was incredibly appealing to my flesh. But it is SO, SO far from God's heart. He revealed the battle plan that was against me and how my flesh liked the thinking the enemy tempted me with! He reminded me that I had to make a choice: agree with thinking that fed my flesh or agree with thinking that is in line with His heart. I want to love what He loves and hate what He hates! He hates critical and judgmental thinking that brings unforgiveness and a breach in relationships.

Whether it be temporary relief of pain in the form of addiction or the pride of self-righteousness, we allow the door to the enemy to remain open as long as we still like the "benefits" the enemy offers more than the path the Father offers us of true comfort, healing, restoration, and freedom. I don't know about you, but I don't want to allow any door—any access to my heart whatsoever—to remain open to the enemy.

Prayer

Father, help me to love what You love and hate what You hate. My freedom in Christ is worth so much more than any so-called "benefit" of the world, my flesh, or the devil. I choose to turn away from my broken preferences and look to Your healing. I want to be whole and complete as You are whole and complete. Father, I ask for Your healing over my thinking. Set me free from old broken places in my thoughts and emotions. I want Your thoughts, and I choose to disagree with the thoughts of the enemy and the "benefits" he offers. I choose Your thoughts and ask You to reveal any place in my mind and emotions where I have allowed agreement with the enemy by liking his "benefits." I choose to put my flesh to death and choose You! Your ways are true comfort! Your heart is for my best! Your path brings me to true life! Amen.

Disagree With the Enemy: How do I change the locks?

A key factor that leads us to forfeit our legal right to freedom is agreement with the lie that God is not good. This pernicious lie keeps us from walking intimately with Him. We don't have to be aware of our agreement with this (or any other) lie for satan to claim his legal right to harass us. Even hidden or implicit agreement can be held against us. So how do you know if you are believing a lie? Often, the struggle is the tell. When we allow ungodly beliefs and lies to remain, we will experience inner conflict. Our spirit, once we have received salvation and positional sanctification, desires to align with the Holy Spirit. The struggle is in the soul realm, where our beliefs and feelings drive our actions. Much of this module is about revealing the struggle and exposing the lies so that you can choose to disagree with the enemy and be truly and legally free.

Sometimes the issue involves quickly recognizing when a thought contradicts the word of God. Several years ago, I (Sally) was listening to a favorite Bible teacher who taught that our thoughts come from three sources: God, our own minds, or the enemy. He explained that if you have an unwanted thought, it is not your thought! In this case, you can quickly let it go without condemnation. An unwanted thought that comes into your mind only becomes yours when you decide to agree with it. For instance, if I have a critical thought towards someone and it shocks me that I could even think like that, it was not my thought. I can and should discard it without feeling any condemnation. Having taken this teaching to heart, these days I sometimes find myself saying, "Oh shut up, enemy; I don't want that thought!" Still, thoughts or suggestions from the enemy can become my thoughts. For instance, when the enemy throws trash in my yard, so to speak, by tempting me with critical thoughts toward someone, I have a choice as to whether I will own responsibility for the trash. If I allow those thoughts to stay in my mind on repeat without taking them captive and throwing them out as the garbage they are, and if I then go on to speak or act out in judgment as a result, then I have allowed that trash to become mine.

This teaching brought me great freedom as I learned to discard thoughts I didn't want to agree with. I learned to recognize that they did not originate with me, and I did not have to beat myself up for them. Choosing to discard, rather than agree with, negative thoughts about God, ourselves, and others, changes the lock on the door so that unwanted squatters cannot get back in.

PRACTICAL APPLICATION

Are you willing now to take some time to talk with the Father and ask Him to identify any "squatters" you may have been putting up with in some way? These squatters have no property rights, but they chatter loudly as though they belong. Is a squatter telling you who you are? Or tormenting you with an area of brokenness or trauma that needs healing? Or might there be a counterfeit "benefit" you've been receiving that you are now willing to trade out for the benefit of real freedom, peace, and joy? Father God is patient, gentle, and kind. You can trust Him to identify what you need most right now. Freedom is a process. We don't "arrive" all at once. You may want to use the following prayer. Repeat as needed:

Father, I ask You to reveal any "squatters" I may have been putting up with in some way. Reveal to me any broken habits and any broken pieces of my identity that You choose to reveal right now. I choose Your rule and reign in my life, and I choose to enforce Your eviction notice. I look to You for forgiveness, healing, and freedom. Forgive me for putting up with "squatters" to whom You have served notice. Help me to love what You love and hate what You hate. Tell me who I am. I choose to agree with what You say about me and to let go of false "benefits." I ask You to heal my heart. Hold me when I am weak and overwhelmed. I want to be whole and complete as You are whole and complete. In the name of Jesus Christ, I pray. Amen.

Forgiveness: But how can I let it go?

Bear with one another and forgive any complaint you may have against someone else. Forgive as the Lord forgave you (Colossians 3:13).

Perhaps the most crucial step to claiming your legal freedom in Christ and walking away from old, painful patterns is to choose forgiveness. Forgiveness is the key that unlocks prison doors and sets captives free. Prisoners are locked up because they have committed a crime. Truly, all have sinned (Romans 3:23) and deserve the death sentence. But God so loved us that He sent Jesus into the world not to condemn us for our sins, but to save us and set us free. God has granted us a pardon for our sins because Jesus took the death penalty on our behalf. All we have to do is acknowledge our need for forgiveness and gratefully receive this extraordinary pardon. Having freely received, we now freely forgive ourselves and others from our hearts.

Forgiveness is a choice we make, not necessarily a feeling. Pride often gets in the way of forgiveness, and it can feel wrong or invalidating to forgive. We aren't suggesting or pretending that it feels good or natural to forgive. Nor are we claiming that it's as easy as following a step-by-step recipe. It's not like you can just assemble the ingredients, measure and combine them in the prescribed way, bake, and presto—you've made forgiveness. Piece of cake. No, sorry. Forgiveness doesn't work like that. Rather, it is a path we choose to walk because Jesus chose to forgive us.

We are not born again knowing how to forgive or having a taste for it. We may still prefer the taste of self-sufficiency, pride, and rebellion. Nevertheless, we must learn to forgive whether we like the idea or not. One key to doing this is to cultivate a deep and daily awareness of how lavish the Father's love is that we should be called children of God (1 John 3:1). We are radically loved despite all the wrongs we have done. Forgiving others is easier when we are mindful of the insurmountable nature of our own sin debt and the prodigality of God's love. Why?

Because those who have been forgiven much, love much (Luke 7:47), and it becomes inconceivable to hold unforgiveness in our hearts toward others.

The sooner we learn the habit of forgiveness, the easier and more automatic it becomes. Just like it's easier to learn languages when we are very young, forgiveness is best learned early in our Christian life. If you feel you're getting a late start, don't worry. It is never too late. By the grace and power of God, you can learn to make forgiveness a part of the rhythm and routine of your daily life with God and others.

PRACTICAL APPLICATION

Then Peter came to Jesus and asked, "Lord, how many times shall I forgive my brother who sins against me? Up to seven times?" Jesus answered, "I tell you, not just seven times, but seventy-seven times! Because of this, the kingdom of heaven is like a king who wanted to settle accounts with his servants. As he began the settlements, a debtor was brought to him owing ten thousand talents. Since the man was unable to pay, the master ordered that he be sold to pay his debt, along with his wife and children and everything he owned. Then the servant fell on his knees before him. 'Have patience with me,' he begged, 'and I will pay back everything.' His master had compassion on him, forgave his debt, and released him. But when that servant went out, he found one of his fellow servants who owed him a hundred denarii. He grabbed him and began to choke him, saying, 'Pay back what you owe me!' So his fellow servant fell down and begged him, 'Have patience with me, and I will pay you back.' But he refused. Instead, he went and had the man thrown into prison until he could pay his debt. When his fellow servants saw what had happened, they were greatly distressed, and they went and recounted all of this to their master. Then the master summoned him and declared, 'You wicked servant! I forgave all your debt because you begged me. Shouldn't you have had mercy on your fellow servant, just as I had on you?' In anger his master turned him over to the jailers to be tortured, until he should repay all that he owed. That is how My heavenly Father will treat each of you unless you forgive your brother from your heart" (Matthew 18:21-35).

A "talent" reflects a unit of money worth about 20 years' wages for a laborer. So how much money did the first servant in this passage owe the master?

10, 000 talents = _____ years' worth of wages

A "denarius" was worth one days' wages for a laborer. So how much money was this same servant owed by his fellow servant?

100 denarii = _____ days' worth of wages

We suggest meditating on the fact that you cannot possibly earn God's love or forgiveness—not in 200,000 years. Let this draw your spirit, heart, and mind into a deeper revelation of the Father's love! We have been forgiven a debt we could never pay. If you have a hard time forgiving others or showing love toward people you'd rather judge, consider this parable and remember how much you are loved and how much you have been forgiven. Doing so will help cultivate humility and soften your heart to forgive and love others in the same manner.

Forgiveness Is a Choice

As a new believer, I (Sally) learned that I must forgive, but nobody really explained how to do it. As a "rubber meets the road" kind of person, I was frustrated. I often felt like I must be really awful because I struggled to forgive. For a few years my husband and I taught Sunday school, and because our church didn't have the funds for curriculum, we had to create our own. I would pray each week about what to teach. One week the Lord put on my heart the story of Lazarus (John 11). As I prepared the lesson, He opened up the story to me in a new way. After Jesus calls Lazarus out of the tomb, He tells those around Him to unbind him. Jesus could have done it, but He chose to tell those around Lazarus to do the work of unbinding him. We, as the body of Christ, are called to help each other get free, to become unbound through the love and power of Jesus.

The day I taught this Sunday school lesson, I went up for prayer at our evening service. The presence of the Lord was powerful, and I had a vision of a hand unbinding me from bandages like those Lazarus may have been bound in. As they were being unwound, they became increasingly dirty. I saw that they were actually being pulled out from within me, from my belly. They began to get so dirty and nasty that they looked gangrenous. At this point, the Holy Spirit showed me a wound from my childhood that I had never dealt with. I had tried to "stuff" it rather than deal with it. Consequently, the wound was still very much present, unhealed, and festering.

As I went home that night, the Lord showed me how this wound had affected many relationships. He showed me that to be healed, I had to forgive. But I had no idea how to do this! This was a very deep and painful wound. I asked the Holy Spirit how to truly forgive. He showed me that forgiveness is not necessarily a feeling, it is a choice. So that night, I prayed, "God, I choose to forgive this person who hurt me." There was no real feeling of forgiveness (although that feeling did come later). I didn't feel much at all, really. But I had been obedient, and that obedience made it possible for healing and freedom to become real in my life. Every time the enemy would try to dredge up the pain, I would take the thoughts captive (I did not want those thoughts!), and say, "I have already chosen to forgive this person. Father, please help me to think on other things—things that are good, pure, and lovely" (Philippians 4:8). When those thoughts came up, I had to remind myself that I had forgiven. I had to take the thoughts captive again. At some point in this process I realized that when the person would come to mind, I no longer felt pain. Forgiveness that began as a choice became more and more authentic, and I experienced true healing and freedom as a result.

The Anesthetic of Grace

My daughter and I (Julie) traveled to South Africa one summer with her evangelical dance team. On the last day of our stay at Michael's Children's Village, we spent the morning on safari. When we got back, we had to pack quickly, say our goodbyes, and get on the road. In my haste to clear off my bottom bunk, I hit my head on the frame and jammed my neck pretty badly. The pain momentarily took my breath away, but I ignored it as best I could and just carried on with the task of packing and leave-taking.

As soon as we got on the road, the pain in my neck demanded my attention. I wanted to ask the team to pray for me, but it wasn't a good time, so I decided to pray silently for a while. As I did, the Lord reminded me of a phrase I'd heard in church the previous day: "the anesthetic of grace." The African pastor had used the phrase in passing and without explanation. Now I asked the Lord to show me what it meant and help me to apply it because I really needed anesthetic!

God answered my request by pouring grace into me rather than by explaining it with words. I felt tangible grace that prompted me to pray for everyone in the van rather than praying for relief from my own pain. I prayed that the "anesthetic of grace" would ease any relational tensions and ease the grief we all felt over leaving the children. I prayed for each member of the team and all they were facing. I don't know how long I prayed, but when I was done, I realized that my neck didn't hurt anymore! The anesthetic of grace had both fueled my prayers for others and eased the physical pain in my neck!

We believe the "anesthetic of grace" can be applied in the process of forgiving those who have hurt us. A pastor once told me that we should forgive until it doesn't hurt anymore and until we can agree in our heart that the person owes us nothing. Without the anesthetic of grace, we easily stay in our pain and anger. It often feels bad and unjust, somehow, to forgive someone who has legitimately wronged us. But grace eases our pain. It reminds us that Jesus knows our grief and sorrow (Isaiah 53:3) and assures us that righteous judgment is in God's hands (Hebrews 10:30).

Forgiveness isn't optional. It is not always easy to forgive, but there is always grace to ease the pain and soothe the wound that may have been bandaged with anger, offense, pride, or self-sufficiency. Grace from God is undeserved favor, help, and kindness. The grace of forgiveness is not something that we get to receive without also giving it to others (as we learned in Matthew 18:21-35). Jesus taught that forgiveness should become a habit of the heart.

Watch yourselves. If your brother sins, rebuke him; and if he repents, forgive him. Even if he sins against you seven times in a day, and seven times returns to say, 'I repent,' you must forgive him (Luke 17:3-4).

Peter asked Jesus if he really had to forgive up to seven times, and Jesus told him not just seven times, but up to seventy times seven (Matthew 18:22)! Discipleship math again. That's up to 490 times a day! What Jesus is saying is that we must forgive as often as necessary. Our freedom depends on this habit of the heart. Forgiveness isn't optional. It sets us free from the pain of offense. We don't have to continue to be hurt, miserable, and angry. Forgiveness isn't punishment or something that just adds insult to injury. No. Forgiveness opens prison doors so that we can walk out.

For if you forgive others their trespasses, your heavenly Father will also forgive you, but if you do not forgive others their trespasses, neither will your Father forgive your trespasses (Matthew 6:14-15, ESV).

PRACTICAL APPLICATION

A Prayer of Forgiveness

The best way to learn to forgive is to choose to forgive. We encourage you to take a moment right now and ask the Lord if there is anyone or anything He wants you to forgive. You may not be ready to forgive those who have hurt you most. But you can start somewhere with something. In using the following prayer, fill in the blanks as specifically as possible.

Lord, I know You want me to forgive _____. So in obedience, I choose to forgive them for what they did that caused my heart to be offended. I declare they owe me nothing. Thank You, Lord, that I can leave this offense with You and release them into the court of heaven. According to Hebrews 10:30, You've said, "Vengeance is Mine; I will repay." You are the righteous judge. I leave judgment of _____ to You. I repent for getting in Your way by trying to do Your job. Thank You, Lord, for freedom from offense. Thank You that as I have forgiven this person, so You have forgiven me. In the name of Jesus Christ, I pray. Amen.

Now, having chosen to forgive, picture your own hurt, anger, and judgment being buried. Or if you prefer, picture a door closing on it. Do not be alarmed if you need to repeat this prayer a few times. The deeper the wound, the longer it may take for your emotions to catch up to your will. But if you are indeed willing to forgive again and again until it doesn't hurt anymore, freedom will come.

Confession and Repentance: Do I have to do this every time?

So if you are offering your gift at the altar and there remember that your brother has something against you, leave your gift there before the altar. First go and be reconciled to your brother; then come and offer your gift (Matthew 5:23-24).

Just as we are called to forgive repeatedly, disciples of Christ are called to repent and receive forgiveness. Most of us better recall the times we have been hurt than the times we have caused hurt. We are more aware of our own pain than someone else's. But we have all wronged others, and we must learn to repent and be forgiven to stay free. We do not want to give the enemy any legal right to torment us.

When my (Julie's) oldest son was three or four years old, I remember his struggle with the concept of repeated repentance. I had observed him doing something mean to his sister, so I took him aside and explained why his actions were unkind and wrong. Then I coached him to say, "I'm sorry for _____. Will you please forgive me?" The first time I required those two sentences I had to wait about 30 minutes before he was willing to say them. We both needed the anesthetic of grace to get through that half hour! A little later that same day I observed him being unkind again. I took him aside and told him he needed to say, "I'm sorry for _____. Will you please forgive me?" He looked at me with a mix of surprise, dismay, and frustration and said, "Mommy, I can't say that *every* time!"

The comment was cute coming from a three-year-old. But coming from a grown child of God, it is less cute. We, too, may think, "I can't do that every time!" But the beauty of our life in Christ is that we don't have to do it on our own. The Holy Spirit enables our repentance even when our own impulse is to resist it. So, let's take a closer look at what it means to repent.

The Greek word for repent is *metanoeó*, pronounced meta-no-way-oh. According to HELPS Word-studies,[19] this compound word comes from *meta*, meaning "changed after being with," and *noiéō*, meaning "to think." So *metanoeó* means "to think differently after being with." Being with whom? Jesus, of course! Apart from Christ, there is no way we can think differently about people or ourselves. But oh! With Christ we can do all things (Philippians 4:13). We can change our thoughts and feelings about ourselves, others, or the situation if we just take a moment with Him. Repentance involves this process of acknowledging that how God thinks is best. There's no way we can think differently on our own. But oh! Right! We aren't on our own, even if we must repent seven times a day for the same offense. It may feel like there's no way to do it. But the Holy Spirit is with us to help us in our weakness, and the anesthetic of grace is available.

---

19 www.biblehub.com

Prayer

Father, repentance doesn't come naturally to me. But I recall Your goodness, grace, and lovingkindness. I am so grateful. Train me, Lord, in the habit of short accounts—to be quick to repent and quick to forgive because of Your great love and mercy. In the name of Jesus Christ, I pray. Amen.

Iniquity Revealed: What hurtful way is hiding in me?

You shall have no other gods before or besides Me. You shall not make yourself any graven image [to worship it] or any likeness of anything that is in the heavens above, or that is in the earth beneath, or that is in the water under the earth; You shall not bow down yourself to them or serve them; for I the Lord your God am a jealous God, visiting the iniquity of the fathers upon the children to the third and fourth generation of those who hate Me, but showing mercy and steadfast love to a thousand generations of those who love Me and keep My commandments (Exodus 20:3-6, AMPC).

One of the major problems we face with iniquity is its ability to hide so well. The very term means "to twist" or "to bend." So iniquity wraps itself around us or embeds itself within us so that we think it's just part of who we are. If we think acting a certain way (for example, bossy) is just our "personality," we will accept certain behavior patterns thinking they are just "who we are" rather than being something (controlling) from which we can and should get free! King David understood this concept. That is why at the end of Psalm 139—that beautiful declaration of praise for how wonderfully God made us—he asks God to search his innermost being and cleanse him from any wickedness or hidden and hurtful way.

Iniquity can be inherited. I (Sally) come from a long line of worriers. Everyone knew my grandma was a worrywart. It was just understood to be a part of who she was. But worry is not a personality trait! I followed in her footsteps, and worry filled my mind and robbed my peace. I could not enjoy the "now" for fear of what might or might not happen in the short- and long-term. Worry is fear projected into the future, and it became an iniquity in my heart, an idol, something I bowed to and let rule me.

These days, Christians don't typically carve idols and place them on the mantle to worship, but we may have idols in our hearts nonetheless. An idol is anything more important to us than God. It is something we spend endless hours serving as it rules over us. Idolatry is prioritizing that thing—whether it is a fear, a goal, a status, another person, or whatever—over God and His kingdom. Any area of rebellion or defiance, any area we have not allowed the Father to cleanse away in a sanctifying bubble bath, may be an area of iniquity and idolatry in our hearts.

For rebellion is as the sin of witchcraft, and stubbornness is as iniquity and idolatry. Because you have rejected the word of the LORD, He also has rejected you from being king (I Samuel 15:23, NKJV).

For rebellion is [as] the sin of divination, and selfwill is [as] iniquity and idolatry. Because thou hast rejected the word of Jehovah, He hath also rejected thee from being king (I Samuel 15:23, Darby).

Thorns and snares are in the way of the obstinate and willful; he who guards himself will be far from them (Proverbs 22:5, AMPC).

Unless you have openly embraced the occult in the past, you might not think of yourself as having opened a door to witchcraft. But according to scripture, stubbornness and rebellion are considered the same as idolatry and witchcraft! We open the door when we choose our ways instead of His because of doubt, unbelief, fear, etc. A spirit of fear nearly always leads to the desire for control. We think that if we are in control we can cope better with our fear and keep bad things from happening. We think we can control people and circumstances, bending them to our will. But exercising this type of fear-based control without a heart surrendered to God is the essence of divination and witchcraft. Why? Because we trust ourselves more than Him. We make ourselves gods. This is the essence of idolatry. Forged in fear, hammered out by the hands of control, the twisted idol of control stands rebelliously and defiantly as a witness to our iniquity.

Fear and the desire to control stem from failing to trust that God loves us and wants the best for us. If we "unpack" it, the lie at the root of our rebellion is that God is not truly good to us. This lie feeds the fear that His outcomes are not good or not what we want. If we truly believed His goodness and love, we would fight less to maintain control. We wouldn't need to be afraid.

Why does God take the iniquity of fear and rebellion so seriously? It's not because He wants us to legalistically follow rules and regulations or work to be perfect, but because He knows that these spirits torment us. Have you ever met a controlling person that exemplified peace? Um, yeah no. The need to control brings torment because it is rooted in the lie that God cannot be trusted. Control allows fear to run rampant. In our experience, people who tend to be legalistic often have issues with control and fear. Legalism puts the focus on performance and control. Legalistic thinking says that if you "perform" in all the correct ways and follow the letter of the law, then God is obligated to bless you. Although there are consequences for our actions, our hope is not in anything we can do. We don't earn His favor. We already have it. This is the wonderful thing called grace! But when we forget to live out of grace, we can easily fall into the idolatry and iniquity of legalism, shame, fear, and control. So what do we do?

For God did not give us a spirit of timidity (of cowardice, of craven and cringing and fawning fear), but [He has given us a spirit] of power and of love and of calm and well-balanced mind and discipline and self-control (2 Timothy 1:7, AMPC).

Often, iniquity will have an "altar," a place where the wounds and pain of the past have been revisited repeatedly and strengthened. Many years ago, the Holy Spirit showed me a vision of a woman I (Sally) knew taking large stones from a river and stacking them on the shore. This woman had walked through some very difficult things and my heart ached for her. Over and over again she went into the river and back. I asked what she was doing and heard, "She is building an altar to her own pain." Then I realized how many old wounds from my past that I, too, had created "altars" for. I would often go back and revisit those wounds, recount them to friends, and think about them repeatedly. They were valid, painful memories. Yet by revisiting them over and over in my head and in conversation, I was only adding stones to the altar. I just relived the pain repeatedly. I asked God to show me where those "altars" were, and the healing process began.

When I was a little girl, I fell off my bike one day. We lived on a gravel road, and some of it got stuck in my knee. I was a bloody mess! My dad sat me down and began to clean the wound and pull out the gravel. It hurt so bad! When he put on the antiseptic, I screamed and begged him to stop. But as a loving, wise father, he gently continued despite my painful protests. He knew it was for my best in the long run. To this day, I have the scars on my knee, and they remind me of my father's love and wisdom.

As with so many things in our walk to freedom, dealing with fear, rebellion, stubbornness, or any other iniquity comes down to making a choice. Do we really want to be healed? Will we trust God with the antiseptic? Will we trust Him for His anesthetic of grace? Although it may not feel great in the moment, can we believe that any momentary pain will be worth it for the healing it brings? I didn't want to have the gravel taken out of my knee, but I trusted my dad. Even more so, we can trust our Heavenly Father to always be working for our good (Romans 8:28).

Prayer

Father, I ask You to come in and show me the hidden things that have tripped me up. I ask You to come in and purge wounds that have become infected. Reveal the hidden iniquity of my heart. Bring to the surface any hurtful way that has kept me from walking in greater freedom in You. I choose not to be afraid. I choose You and Your loving ways over fear. I want to be well! In the name of Jesus Christ, I pray. Amen!

Self-protective Habits that Hinder Freedom: Am I blocking my own progress?

When we feel hurt or threatened, the natural response is to protect ourselves. Unfortunately, in the context of spiritual freedom, when self-protective responses become habits, they can end up doing us more harm than good. They may seem good and effective initially, keeping us from further harm in the same way a cast protects a broken leg. But if we stay in the cast too long and refuse to face the temporary pain of learning to walk again, we will become crippled. Just as rehab to recover from a bad break or sprain is often necessary, it is common for us to need help recovering from the cast and crutches we've long relied on to protect our hearts. In this section, we address three common self-protective strategies that, over time, become crippling and counterproductive because they prevent us from freely relating to God and to others who love us. The strategies we address include (1) building walls around our hearts, (2) making inner vows or promises to ourselves, and (3) judging others out of bitterness and resentment.

Walls

Surely the arm of the LORD is not too short to save, nor His ear too dull to hear. But your iniquities have built barriers between you and your God, and your sins have hidden His face from you, so that He does not hear (Isaiah 59:1-2)

Sometimes we feel like God doesn't hear us. It's like our prayers hit a brick wall and bounce back unheard and unattended. But Isaiah assures us that the problem is not with God. He's not dull of hearing or lacking in any way. The problem is the barrier we have built. We don't necessarily do it intentionally or with conscious awareness, but many of us build walls of self-protection around our hearts to prevent further pain. The problem is these walls are self-serving idols; they are altars of self-reliance that memorialize pain instead of resolving it. Walls also shut God and others out. Our walls create the illusion that God cannot hear, but the problem is the barrier around our hearts, not Him.

Our walls grieve the heart of the Father who longs to protect and comfort us. According to scripture, we do not need them because God is our fortress. We are invited to run to Him for protection. He is our shield and an ever-present help in times of trouble. Here are just a few examples that reveal God as our protector:

The LORD is a refuge for the oppressed, a stronghold in times of trouble (Psalm 9:9).

God is our refuge and strength, an ever-present help in times of trouble (Psalm 46:1).

He who dwells in the shelter of the Most High will abide in the shadow of the Almighty. I will say to the LORD, "You are my refuge and my fortress, my God, in whom I trust" (Psalm 91:1-2).

Blessed be the LORD, my Rock, who trains my hands for war, and my fingers for battle. He is my steadfast love and my fortress, my stronghold and my deliverer. He is my shield, in whom I take refuge, who subdues peoples under me (Psalm 144:1-2).

He alone is my rock and my salvation; He is my fortress; I will not be shaken (Psalm 62:6).

I love you, O LORD, my strength. The LORD is my rock, my fortress, and my deliverer. My God is my rock, in whom I take refuge, my shield, and the horn of my salvation, my stronghold. I will call upon the LORD, who is worthy to be praised; so shall I be saved from my enemies (Psalm 18:1-3).

The LORD is good, a stronghold in the day of distress; He cares for those who trust in Him (Nahum 1:7).

"Because of the devastation of the afflicted, because of the groaning of the needy,

Now I will arise," says the LORD; "I will place him in the safety for which he longs" (Psalm 12:5, AMP).

Did you catch that last one? The Lord promises to place us in the safety for which we long. Therefore, we have no real need for self-protection. When we throw up walls around our hearts and harden them against pain, people, and God (Ephesians 4:17-18), we may feel safer momentarily, but in the long run, we suffer more. With thick and impenetrable walls, no one can get in to love us, and we can't get out of ourselves to love others, either. Just as stagnant water is a breeding ground for bacteria, a stagnant and blocked-off heart will make us sick because we need love to flow both into and out of our hearts.

PRACTICAL APPLICATION

Over time, the barriers of self-protection we build hinder freedom and intimacy with the One who loves us best. If you have hidden behind a self-protective barrier, are you willing to let your guard down before God and/or someone else you can trust? You don't have to trust everyone all at once, but you can be sure that the Father loves you. *But whoever listens to me will dwell in safety, secure from the fear of evil* (Proverbs 1:33).

Lord, I confess that I have put up a wall around my heart in an effort to protect myself from pain. Forgive me for my self-reliance and pride in thinking that I don't need You. Thank You for Your promise to love me and never to leave me or forsake me (Deuteronomy 31:6). You are my God in whom I trust. Be my fortress and my deliverer. Set me free to love and be loved. Thank You for pouring Your love into my heart even now (Romans 5:5). In the name of Jesus Christ, I pray. Amen.

Inner Vows

Inner vows are the oaths we utter and the promises we make to ourselves in moments of pain, anger, grief, or betrayal. Such vows are rooted in pride and the presumption that we have what it takes to keep them. They assume self-sufficiency and indicate agreement with the lie that we have the power and ability to protect ourselves. Ironically, inner vows keep us in a cycle of pain (see page 144) and bondage. We spend energy on self-protection rather than on pursuing who we are in Christ. Often, inner vows are counter-productive, resulting in the very thing we are trying to avoid. For example, when you vow not to be like the person who hurt you, you are likely to become more like this person as time goes on. (We explain this further in the next section on bitter-root judgments.)

Do not be quick to speak, and do not be hasty in your heart to utter a word before God. After all, God is in heaven and you are on earth. So let your words be few (Ecclesiastes 5:2).

It is better not to vow than to make a vow and not fulfill it (Ecclesiastes 5:5).

But I say to you, Do not take an oath at all, either by heaven, for it is the throne of God, or by the earth, for it is his footstool, or by Jerusalem, for it is the city of the great King. And do not take an oath by your head, for you cannot make one hair white or black. Let what you say be simply 'Yes' or 'No'; anything more than this comes from evil (Matthew 5:34-37, ESV).

But above all, my brothers, do not swear, either by heaven or by earth or by any other oath, but let your "yes" be yes and your "no" be no, so that you may not fall under condemnation (James 5:12, ESV).

PRACTICAL APPLICATION

We encourage you to take a moment to read over the following list of common inner vows. Do any of them sound familiar?

I will NEVER let anyone love me.
I will NEVER be weak.
I will NEVER trust anyone.
I will NEVER allow myself to need anything from anybody.
I will NEVER let them take anything away from me.
I will NEVER allow anyone to touch me.
I will NEVER share what is mine.
I will NEVER allow anyone to give me money.

I will NEVER go out at night.
I will NEVER let you see who I am.
I will NEVER let anyone know when I'm hurting.
I will NEVER let anyone control or influence me.
I will NEVER be responsible for other people.
I will NEVER be able to receive a compliment.
I will NEVER enjoy life.
I will NEVER allow anyone into my heart.
I will NEVER be anything worthwhile.
I will ALWAYS be independent and self-sufficient.
I will ALWAYS be logical.
I will ALWAYS be in control of my life.
I will ALWAYS protect myself.
I will ALWAYS make others prove they love me
I will ALWAYS have the right answer.
I will ALWAYS anticipate problems before they happen.

If you have identified any inner vows, we offer the following prayer as an aid to renouncing them and breaking their spiritual, legal hold on you.

Prayer to Break Inner Vows

*Lord, I confess that in my pain and woundedness, I vowed _____.
I knowingly (or unknowingly) chose to believe the lie that I could protect myself. I responded with self-sufficiency, pride, and independence. I choose now to repent and renounce this vow in the name of Jesus Christ. In doing so, I let go of every false sense of protection, power, independence, control, and vindication that it gave me. Thank You for Your forgiveness. Thank You that I am free now. Help me walk in the joy and peace of believing You, Lord, for protection and loving connection. Help me learn how to love as well as how to feel and be loved. In the name of Jesus Christ, I pray. Amen.*

Bitter-root Judgments

Do not be deceived: God is not mocked, for whatever one sows, that will he also reap. For the one who sows to his own flesh will from the flesh reap corruption, but the one who sows to the Spirit will from the Spirit reap eternal life (Galatians 6:7-8, ESV).

See to it that no one falls short of the grace of God, and that no root of bitterness springs up to cause trouble and defile many (Hebrews 12:15).

The principle of sowing and reaping means that whatever kind of seed we plant and water determines the kind of fruit we will eventually harvest. When we sow seed to our flesh apart from Christ, the harvest we get is corruption and death. But if we are faithful to plant seeds in the Spirit, we will reap the fruit of righteousness. We may be familiar with this principle, but so is the enemy—and he doesn't play fair. He will use it against us whenever possible. He loves to sow seeds of pain and confusion early in life which can grow into deep roots of bitterness, disappointment, and unforgiveness—all of which produce an unrighteous, poisonous harvest. This is why Paul models forgiveness and urges the Corinthians to forgive as well. He does not want the enemy to outwit them through unforgiveness (2 Corinthians 2:10-11).

Judgments, in general, are the conclusions we come to about God, ourselves, or others. A "bitter-root judgment" is a conclusion produced by the seed of pain that has been allowed to grow into a deep root of bitterness. Such roots create a world of hurt if we refuse to forgive and continue to allow them to grow unchecked. They begin as a response to pain, and that pain can quickly lead to anger, resentment, or criticism. Bitter-root judgments can lead us into thinking bad outcomes are inevitable, make us jaded, cause us to judge the hearts of others, and choke out the grace we need to allow ourselves and others to grow and change. Inevitably, if we allow bitter roots to fester and grow, the enemy will have the legal right to multiply unrighteousness (Hosea 8:7). For this reason, we need to practice being quick to turn to the Lord in our pain. Quick to forgive. Quick to allow the Holy Spirit to help us in our weakness. When we refuse the grace of forgiveness, it's like fertilizing the bitter root, and it will grow very quickly.

To illustrate, let's say that someone unkindly and unfairly called you ugly or stupid when you were a child. The pain of this verbal rejection may have sunk in and germinated in your soul as a bitter root. Unequipped to forgive, you protected your heart with anger and unforgiveness which turned to bitterness and resentment. Without the tools or teaching on forgiveness, you learned to protect yourself from further pain using quick sarcasm, criticism, and judgment of others. This dynamic usually has two aspects. First, the seed of rejection produces the belief that others are always judging you, and this ungodly belief results in you being quick to "see" rejection even where none exists. Second, you become more likely to judge others. For example, you may find yourself noticing others' lack of beauty or brains and making snarky comments, not even realizing that you're speaking out of your own woundedness and pain.

What we really need is to tend our hearts like a garden. Rather than letting the weeds of unforgiveness, anger, disappointment, and pain grow unchecked, we can ask the Lord to help us pull them up and out. That way we are free to grow in beauty, and the weeds will not spread into our neighbor's garden.

PRACTICAL APPLICATION

Remember, becoming free INDEED is a process that begins when we allow the Lord to identify an area He wants to address. So, whenever the Holy Spirit makes us aware of a bitter root or an ungodly belief or a seed of unforgiveness, the best response is to thank Him for having identified the root. Then we can repent and renounce any way in which we've agreed with the enemy. The Holy Spirit will only bring an issue to our attention if there is a real and immediate offer of freedom. Take it! Our repentance shows that we acknowledge our need for change. Our repentance is an act of disagreement with the enemy. We can now, with authority, evict the spirit of bitterness, anger, unforgiveness, judgment, or whatever. When we exalt the Lord, the devil will flee (James 4:7). Then we can declare our freedom in Christ and our steadfast commitment to walk in His ways.

You, therefore, have no excuse, you who pass judgment on another. For on whatever grounds you judge the other, you are condemning yourself, because you who pass judgment do the same things. And we know that God's judgment against those who do such things is based on truth (Romans 2:1-2).

Do not judge, or you will be judged. For with the same judgment you pronounce, you will be judged; and with the measure you use, it will be measured to you (Matthew 7:1-2).

Do not judge, and you will not be judged. Do not condemn, and you will not be condemned. Forgive, and you will be forgiven. Give, and it will be given to you. A good measure, pressed down, shaken together, and running over will be poured into your lap. For with the measure you use, it will be measured back to you (Luke 6:37-38).

Make sure there is no man or woman, clan or tribe among you today whose heart turns away from the LORD our God to go and worship the gods of those nations. Make sure there is no root among you that bears such poisonous and bitter fruit (Deuteronomy 29:18).

Prayer to Release Bitterness and Judgment

Father, in the name of Jesus Christ, I choose this day to renounce and repent of agreeing with bitterness and judgment toward _____. I take responsibility and ask You to break the power of bitterness, criticism, and judgment in my life and through my generations. I ask for Your forgiveness, and I receive Your forgiveness. I ask You to heal any area in my spirit, soul, or body that may have been affected by the bitterness, unforgiveness, and judgments I have held toward_____. I ask You to bring complete healing in Jesus' name. I thank You for forgiveness, and I ask You to destroy the bad fruit that has already grown out of my bitter-root judgments. Let there be a crop failure, Lord. I choose the fruit of love, joy, peace, patience, kindness, goodness, faithfulness, gentleness, and self-control (Galatians 5:22-23). Thank You, Holy Spirit, for producing in me a harvest of righteousness from this day forward. In the name of Jesus Christ, I pray. Amen.

Relational Idolatry/Ungodly Soul Ties: Is someone bringing you down?

The term "soul ties" is used by those who do inner-healing and deliverance ministry to refer to the ungodly bonds that form between people. We think of ungodly soul ties as a type of idolatry, specifically relational idolatry. It develops when someone to whom we are connected comes to have a greater impact on our mental and/or emotional well-being than God. This connection may be experienced as positive or negative, but when the connection is "off," when it is ungodly in some way, it gets in the way of our ability to hear and respond to Father God. When this happens, we are in for trouble.

As with many things, the enemy will twist what is good and right and do his best to make it unholy. So it is with human attachments. Everyone needs to experience loving attachments to others. We are born with a healthy need to bond with our parents/caregivers, and there is nothing wrong with that.

In fact, our brains are wired to help us form those bonds, and we never grow out of the need for them. Connection contributes to our mental, emotional, and physical health.[20] For this reason, not all attachments are ungodly. It is good to enjoy healthy, secure connections with parents or children, siblings, a spouse, and close friends. For example, scripture speaks of the godly soul tie between David and Jonathan:

As soon as he had finished speaking to Saul, the soul of Jonathan was knit to the soul of David, and Jonathan loved him as his own soul (1 Samuel 18:1, ESV).

In describing the friendship between David and Jonathan, scripture says nothing that would suggest that the relationship was idolatrous or displeasing to God. Rather, it is a beautiful picture of sacrificial brotherly love.

But even relationships that are healthy can get skewed and ungodly. This happens when we come to love and value the relationship more than we love God. Unhealthy attachments can develop between friends, dating couples, siblings, parents and children, pastors and parishioners, therapists and clients, etc. Any relationship can get "off." In some cases, the ungodly nature of the relationship is obvious, as with a physically or emotionally abusive spouse. But relational idolatry/ungodly soul ties can be subtle, too, as when you care more about someone's opinion than about what God is telling you. As always, we need the Lord to identify when there is an issue because when ungodly soul ties exist, satan has the legal right to harass us. And as we've seen, he loves to press any advantage.

Besides ungodly mental and emotional attachments, another category of relational idolatry/ungodly soul ties are formed based on sexual intimacy.

Do you not know that your bodies are members of Christ? Shall I then take the members of Christ and make them members of a prostitute? Never! Or do you not know that he who is joined to a prostitute becomes one body with her? For, as it is written, "The two will become one flesh." But he who is joined to the Lord becomes one spirit with him. Flee from sexual immorality. Every other sin a person commits is outside the body, but the sexually immoral person sins against his own body. Or do you not know that your body is a temple of the Holy Spirit within you, whom you have from God? You are not your own, for you were bought with a price. So glorify God in your body (1 Corinthians 6:15-20, ESV).

---

20 Brannon, L., Updegraff, J. A., & Feist, J. (2022). *Health Psychology: An Introduction to Behavior and Health, 10th edition.* Boston, MA: Cengage.

The implications of this scripture are clear and profound, and there is no easy way to put it. A soul tie exists between you and every person with whom you have had sexual relations, meaning any activity that arouses you or your partner to lust. By definition, lust is a very strong sexual desire. Jesus taught that even thinking about and lusting after someone in your heart is wrong (Matthew 5:28). Thus, if you are not married and you engage in activities that arouse strong sexual desire in you and/or your partner, you are creating ungodly soul ties. The giving and taking of sexual pleasure are reserved for the covenant of marriage. Indulging prematurely creates unholy physical and mental/emotional ties between partners. Such ties provide satan with legal grounds to harass and oppress you. Sex is a beautiful thing within the covenant of marriage, but there is no getting around the fact that sexual intimacy outside of marriage is idolatry. It is placing the person and/or the pleasure above God. Thus, if you have not taken the time to confess, repent, and renounce these soul ties, satan has legal grounds to torment you.

The good news is that relational idolatry and the soul ties they create can be renounced and severed. Once broken, the enemy no longer has the right to condemn you for them (Romans 8:1-2). In the next Practical Application, we have written a prayer to guide you in renouncing relational idolatry and breaking ungodly soul ties. Prayerfully consider if there is one or more persons from whom you need to make a break, someone who is more important and/or has more power over your emotional well-being than the Lord. You may need to break soul ties with a sexual partner (or multiple partners) or renounce mental/emotional ties with past dating partners, friends, or even a family member. You will be amazed at how much freedom and relief you can experience once you do the work of renouncing relational idolatry.

But before we get to the practical application, there is another type of idolatry/ungodly soul tie we need to explain. This is the soul tie that can exist between our soul (thoughts, emotions, and will) and demonic or ungodly spirits (such as fear, pride, anger, shame, etc.). These kinds of soul ties often develop because of coping mechanisms adopted when we were young. For example, to cope with the pain of unmet love needs, we may partner with the spirit of pride which tells us that we do not need anyone. Or to cope with rejection, we may partner with a spirit of anger that pushes people away and promises to keep us emotionally "safe" from more rejection. Agreement/attachment with ungodly spirits such as these can be dealt with similarly to soul ties with people. We must sever the "relationship" we have with the ungodly spirit and reaffirm our reliance on God alone to meet the needs of our spirit, soul, and body (Exodus 20:3).

The first step to getting free is—as always—to ask the Lord to identify any potential ungodly attachments or any relationships (past or present) that have been more important to us than God. Next, we acknowledge that we need the blood of Jesus to cover the sin that led us into that ungodly bond. By the power of the cross, we come out of agreement with whatever is unhealthy and ungodly in the relationship and evict any ungodly spirit attached to it. Having broken legal agreement with what is ungodly, we ask the Lord to help us establish healthy relationships and godly attachments. We continue to work on getting free from whatever ungodly thing the Lord shows us, and we continue to develop the habit of exalting the Lord and declaring our freedom in Christ.

PRACTICAL
APPLICATION

If you have never heard about soul ties before, you may be feeling a little overwhelmed or even sick to your stomach. That's okay. Remember the Father's heart is for you, and there is no condemnation for those who are in Christ Jesus. Allow the anesthetic of grace to soothe you and give you the strength you need. You may even want to make a list of individuals with whom you must renounce and break soul ties. Then use the following prayer to do just that. We recommend, if possible, that you go somewhere private where you can pray out loud. You are taking a stand against satan, the prince of the power of the air (Ephesians 2:2), and he needs to hear you mean business! (We know someone who took their list and this prayer into an open field and shouted!)

Prayer to Renounce Relational Idolatry and Break Ungodly Soul Ties

Father, by an act of my will and with the help of the Holy Spirit, I repent of and renounce relational idolatry. I ask for Your forgiveness, and I receive Your forgiveness in Jesus' name. I choose now to break all ungodly, unholy, and unhealthy soul ties with _____. I reject, renounce, and sever every unholy influence of this soul tie on my thoughts, my emotions, my will, and my behavior. I confess that because of this idolatry, an unholy exchange of identity, purpose, heart, soul, and mind took place between _____ and myself. I lost part of myself, and I took something that never belonged to me. So now in the name of Jesus Christ, I give back to _____ what was never mine to take and declare that I no longer need or want those things. And I take back the things that are mine washed in the blood of Jesus. Thank You for forgiving me completely, Lord Jesus, and for completely restoring the foundations of my identity and purpose in You. It's not too late. Thank You that according to Your word in Isaiah 61, You give me beauty in exchange for these relational ashes. I thank You that I no longer have to walk in any measure of guilt or shame. Instead, You give me a double portion of honor and everlasting joy. I exalt Your name, Father God, and declare that You are good, and You do good (Psalm 119:68). In the name of Jesus Christ, I pray. Amen.

Battles in the Spirit Realm: Do I need freedom from demonic torment?

"The scriptural way to see things is to set the Lord always before us, put Christ in the center of our vision, and if Satan is lurking around he will appear on the margin only and be seen as but a shadow on the edge of the brightness. It is always wrong to reverse this—to set Satan in the focus of our vision and push God out to the margin. Nothing but tragedy can come of such inversion … The best way to keep the enemy out is to keep Christ in … It is not the praying sheep Satan fears but the presence of the shepherd."

~A. W. Tozer, *Born After Midnight*

Tozer reminds us that Christ is our priority and should remain the center of our attention and pursuit. Christ's death and resurrection guarantees our inheritance as children of God. We are not slaves to sin and death! Jesus purchased the deed to our freedom and declares us truly free! That said, learning to recognize ways in which we have agreed with the enemy's lies about God and ourselves is vitally important because the enemy doesn't play fair. Many of our misconceptions originate in childhood, and our response patterns (habits) get established like well-worn paths or ruts down the side of a hill. Like water, we typically take the path of least resistance unless we are intentional about change. Changing habits requires effort and persistence. To be free indeed requires a willingness to battle in the soul realm, in our thoughts, emotions, and choices.

But we must also recognize that another kingdom is at war against the kingdom of God (Ephesians 6:12). The negative experiences we go through as children and young adults can and often do provide a point of access, an open door, for evil spirits to afflict us. In other words, our battles are not just in the soul realm, but also in the spiritual realm. Given access to our thoughts, emotions, and will, evil spirits will gladly torment us. Christians cannot be "owned" or "possessed" by the enemy, but demons may be hiding in our flesh and need to be evicted.[21] Rather than being afraid of demons, we need to learn how to take our stand against the enemy's schemes and wage war against spiritual forces of evil in the heavenly realm. Fortunately, the weapons of our warfare are suited to the battle (2 Corinthians 10:4). Our part is to learn when and how to wield them.

To illustrate, my (Sally's) family line is rife with rejection. I learned the thought patterns of rejection through observation and experience. The trauma I experienced from various rejection events opened the door to a spiritual attachment, to a spirit of rejection. Initially, I didn't even know that there was a spirit of rejection at work that I needed to fight, let alone know how to fight it with "weapons of warfare." Because I didn't know any better, a stronghold was created involving both soul (mind, will, emotions) and spirit. Often we unknowingly give access to ungodly spirits through what is familiar, things we have learned are "normal."

This analogy illustrates my point: For someone who grew up in middle-class suburbia, someone knocking on the door at 2:00 am would arouse suspicion and alarm. But if you grew up in the inner city with a drug dealer parent, a knock on the door in the middle of the night might be "normal." You may even have been told to open the door any time, day or night, or you'd get in trouble. We learn what is "normal" by our environment and by what we are taught. Consequently, we unconsciously accept or reject things in our lives based on what we've learned. Many people we have ministered to over the years, individuals who have suffered terrible abuse as children, have told us that they didn't even realize what they were experiencing was wrong or abnormal until well into adulthood. Oftentimes, it's not until they got to know other people and saw how they live that they came to understand that something in their family was not right.

As for our battles in the spiritual realm, we do not believe that those who are in Christ can be "possessed" by an evil spirit. However, we believe scripture is clear that a believer can be bothered, tempted, harassed, tormented, and oppressed by the enemy. To be oppressed means to be burdened with

---

21 "Possessed" is an unfortunate translation of a Greek word that means "demonized." The enemy does not own believers, but we can be harassed and tormented. This torment takes place in our soul and our body. Thus, we need to learn to cast demonic spirits out of the temple of our body and close any access points in our mind and emotions.

cruel or unjust impositions or restraints, to be subjected to a burdensome or harsh exercise of authority or power, and to be weighed down by thoughts or feelings that lie heavily on the mind or spirit. The good news is we do not have to put up with demonic oppression!

When He had disarmed the rulers and authorities [those supernatural forces of evil operating against us], He made a public example of them [exhibiting them as captives in His triumphal procession], having triumphed over them through the cross (Colossians 2:15, AMP).

As we have discussed, we were created as triune beings—spirit, soul, and body. We have a spirit redeemed through Jesus' work on the cross, a soul in need of renewal and restoration, and a body in need of yielding. Consequently, we need to treat each aspect differently in our quest to be free indeed. An evil spirit that comes to create havoc within us needs to be rejected as an unwelcome squatter and "cast out" (Mark 9:25, Matthew 17:18, Luke 11:14). You cannot reason with a demon or ask it politely to leave! In contrast, counsel, understanding, and comfort can work wonders for our soul (mind, heart, will). Unhealthy soul patterns are overcome by renewing and restoring our minds (Romans 12:2, Titus 3:5, AMP), allowing our hearts to be healed (Romans 5:5; Ephesians 3:16-19), and consistently choosing God's way (Philippians 2:12-13; Ephesians 4:1). Finally, our bodies need to be disciplined (1 Corinthians 9:27). You cannot cast out flesh or reason it away!

Although demons can harass believers and nonbelievers alike, followers of Christ have been given authority over all the power of the enemy (Luke 10:19). We don't have to put up with harassing spirits. We can bind them and cast them out in Jesus' name. But one of the things I (Sally) have struggled with in the past is how to tell the difference between a learned behavior pattern or negative mindset (that is, a struggle in my soul) versus a struggle with an evil spiritual force behind it. In my experience, if I seemed unable to get victory over something even after using all the tools I had acquired through my study of the word, this usually meant there was a demonic root or stronghold that needed to be addressed.

For instance, I was plagued with night terrors and horrific dreams before I came to Jesus. As I grew in my faith, I learned to pray when fears started to rise in me. I learned to take thoughts captive. I memorized and quoted many verses on overcoming fear with the love and power of God. Yet I was still tormented with sleep paralysis, severe nightmares, and loads of fear in general. It turned out I had many layers of fear spirits that had come in through traumatic childhood events. I needed deliverance. Deliverance didn't completely replace the battle in my mind, will, and emotions, but it was an absolutely vital component in my journey to freedom. As I experienced deliverance, the sleep paralysis and nightmares stopped. I can now recognize fear's tactics far quicker and with much more clarity, so I am able to take the thoughts captive and cut off access immediately.

Scripture is very clear that fear can come as a spirit, not just an emotion:

For God did not give us a spirit of timidity or cowardice or fear, but [He has given us a spirit] of power and of love and of sound judgment and personal discipline [abilities that result in a calm, well-balanced mind and self-control] (2 Tim 1:7, AMP).

There is no fear in love; but perfect love casts out fear, because fear involves torment. But he who fears has not been made perfect in love (1 John 4:18, NKJV).

As we have tried to emphasize, we need the Lord to help us identify the struggle, including whether it is in the spiritual realm or in our mind/ will/emotions. There is no substitute for praying for discernment and revelation. But it is likely that at some point you will need help. Remember, Jesus told those standing around Lazarus to unbind him. We need each other on this journey. It is helpful to be able to recognize the signs of demonic activity when trying to walk out your freedom and/or when trying to help unbind someone else. Because we have been given the authority of Christ to resist the devil (James 4:7) and cast out demons (Mark 16:17; Luke 10:19), we need not be afraid. Rather, we can be bold "bouncers" in the spirit, enforcing the rule and reign of the kingdom of God in our lives.

When to Suspect Demonic Activity

1. **Any previous involvement with the occult** (Deuteronomy 18:10; Leviticus 19:31). This could include any experiences with fortune telling, seances/necromancy (consulting the dead), tarot cards, idols, ancestral worship, Wicca, astral projection, spirit guides, transcendental meditation, nature worship, Ouija boards, horoscopes, New Age modalities, etc. Taking part in occultic behavior is a wide-open door to the demonic. When you open that door, intentionally or not, demonic infestation is inevitable.

2. **Refusing to forgive.** Forgiveness for the Christian is not an option, it is a

requirement (Matthew 6:12; 18:34-35). Refusal to forgive is a clear disregard of scripture and gives the enemy access and a legal right to torment us. Refusing to forgive is choosing the ways of the world, self, and the enemy over the ways of Jesus.

3. Severe trauma. Traumatic events, especially when they occur in childhood, can open doors to demonic harassment because, in our pain and confusion, the enemy comes in with lies and false comfort. We need the truth to displace the lies. We need to open our hearts to being healed by a loving God.

4. Extreme fatigue/sleepiness/yawning/lack of focus when trying to read the Bible, pray, or go to church. We all get sleepy while reading from time to time, but if you experience a pronounced and sudden fatigue when you are not tired, this may be a sign of demonic activity (Matthew 26:40).

5. Intrusive thoughts and voices that you are unable to silence. We all battle thoughts we don't want from time to time. Although we can take our thoughts captive and renew our minds with God's word, the enemy will still try to plant demonic thoughts in our minds. These intrusive thoughts are intense and difficult to combat. For example, obsessive/compulsive thoughts, aggressive thoughts of self-harm and self-hatred, perverse thoughts, or judgmental thoughts about God and others—all of these are from the father of lies (John 8:44).

6. Fear. One way to tell the difference between fear as a natural or emotional response and fear as a spirit is when it feels so overwhelming that you cannot function. A spirit of fear can cause you to freeze up or feel panicked and unable to breathe, even if there is no present danger. Fear as an emotion is temporary (see Module 4). Fear spirits persist in their torment (1 John 4:18).

7. Chronic heaviness/depression. If you feel gripped by an overwhelming sense of heaviness, hopelessness, and/or depression that feels insurmountable, especially when there is no apparent reason for it, it may be a spirit of darkness (Isaiah 61:3).

8. Paranormal experiences. If you have felt an unexplained presence, things moving or turning on and off, shadow people, energies, like something tripped you on purpose, etc., such experiences are indicative of the presence of demons (Ephesians 6:12).

9. Chronic illness. Although sickness can simply be in the natural realm, it can also be indicative of demonic activity (Luke 4:38-40). If you suspect demonic involvement, follow the practical guidance of James 5:14-16 and James 4:7-8.

10. Emotional reactions out of proportion to the situational trigger. When we react to people or situations with more anger, disgust, disappointment, despair, or helplessness than is truly warranted by the situation, there is almost always something hidden that is fueling the intensity. It may only be unprocessed pain and trauma, but more often there is a demonic attachment that amplifies our reactions. The enemy loves to use our pain as an access point for creating even more pain and torment.

11. Struggling to pray, loss of spiritual desire/pulling away from other Christians. Did you once have a vibrant prayer life and desire to study and learn the word but now find yourself struggling to spend time with Him and disinterested in learning more in the word? Have you begun to isolate yourself from other friends who are believers (Proverbs 18:1)? Or, as a newer believer, do you find distractions abound and your desire to pray and to learn more about Him waning? These signs can all be indications of spiritual attack.

Often we have lived with issues for so long we are not even aware of the problem, let alone the demonic root. In the following sections we address issues of shame, rejection, and fear. These are very common strongholds all of which are typically rooted in the lie that we are abandoned, orphaned, and alone. To get free usually requires doing battle in the spirit first and then following up with discipline and commitment in both body and soul.

The Abandonment Lie: Is this my problem?

Scripture makes it clear that much of the battle we face is not against other people but against spiritual forces of evil in the heavenly realm (Ephesians 6:12). This truth is evident from the beginning. Eve didn't battle against Adam, she battled (and lost) against the father of lies. When Adam and Eve disobeyed by choosing independence…choosing to eat the fruit for the "benefit" of the knowledge of good and evil…they got what they were after: The experiential knowledge of good and evil. Suddenly they knew the devastating effects of being disconnected from God. Their disobedience left them painfully aware of evil and feeling utterly alone and vulnerable. Goodness had covered them. Evil now stripped them of innocence and left them naked, ashamed, and afraid.

The pattern holds today. Feeling alone and abandoned leaves us vulnerable to spirits of shame, rejection, and fear. In our own personal experience and in our ministry experience, we have seen that shame and rejection, although distinguishable, are essentially evil twin sisters birthed out of a spirit of abandonment. Fear, too, is spawned by that same lying spirit that tells us we are alone and unloved (1 John 4:18). This is why we have tried to emphasize the goodness of God and the need to settle it in our hearts that He is good. He never leaves us nor forsakes us (Deuteronomy 31:6; Hebrews 13:5). We are not desolate orphans left with no comfort, we are chosen and adopted (John14:18, Ephesians 1:5). His perfect love casts out fear and speaks a better word than rejection or shame. In His great love, Jesus canceled the deadly effects of humanity's disobedience through His obedience. Although innocent and sinless, He suffered the same devastating consequence of sin—being utterly forsaken by God and alone (see Mark 15:34). Paradoxically, by suffering the same abandonment as Adam and Eve, He canceled the effects of their disobedience and made it possible, once again, for humanity to experience unbroken fellowship with the good, good God who loves us. We battle from a position of victory through the death and resurrection of Jesus Christ!

Shame

Shame is an intensely painful emotion associated with moral or performance failure. Shame damages our feelings of self-worth and is often accompanied by an experience of humiliation, loss of respect, and/or damage to self-image. Not surprisingly, we often respond to shaming events with defensive pride that serves to protect our wounded sense of self. We have expressions in English like "the blush of shame" and "hot with shame" that communicate the pain we feel when we are self-conscious with shame. Shame is different from guilt. Guilt is about behavior. It is what we feel when we have done something wrong, and it motivates us to try to make things right. In contrast, shame is about identity. Whereas guilt says we did something bad, shame says we are something bad.

Shame is a universal experience. All have sinned. No one is perfect. Everyone is guilty of both moral and performance failures, and shame is a normal human emotional response in such situations. But for some of us, shame can become an area of spiritual bondage (a stronghold). In other words, a demonic spirit of shame can torment us. As we've seen, the enemy doesn't play fair, and he attacks us when we are young and unable to recognize his schemes. Shame becomes a spiritual stronghold when we habitually agree with the lie that we are worthless and unlovable. Over time, shame can become so deeply embedded in our self-understanding that we end up, paradoxically, sabotaging and hurting ourselves rather than effectively protecting ourselves from further psychological and emotional damage. When we believe shame's message that we are bad, that we don't deserve to be happy, that we aren't good enough or even worthy of the air we breathe, then life takes on a shame-tinged hue. It distorts everything as we view life through the worm's-eye perspective. Such chronic shame is destructive and toxic.

That is not to say that as an emotion shame is inherently sinful. It isn't (see Module 4). Rather, shame can function to motivate us to restore our standing and connection with others. For example, after King David's spectacular moral failure involving adultery, intrigue, and murder (see 2 Samuel 11), the Lord confronted his sin through the prophet Nathan. David was deeply ashamed. Rather than trying to hide or blame-shift, David admitted and confessed his sin and then wrote a song of repentance (Psalm 51) in which he prays for forgiveness and restoration (v. 12). Thus, David provides us with a remarkable example of how to deal with shame without being devastated or incapacitated by either a worm's eye or a bird's eye view of himself. He did not get defensive or allow shame and pride (which are two sides of the same coin) to blind him to the truth. Instead, he chose to agree with God and repent of his moral failure.

Nathan was both a messenger from the Lord and a friend to David. His input provided a safe context in which David could repent and be restored. Often, however, we do not have the benefit of a safe relationship or context. Without that, shame quickly leads to the impulse to hide. For example, if people laugh at us when we fail, we won't feel safe trying again. And even if there is real safety—as with God—if we don't believe we're safe, we will have a broken, fig-leaf response. In the garden, after Adam and Eve ate the forbidden fruit, they became aware of their moral failure and responded by hiding behind fig leaves. They were still safe with God, but they didn't realize it. They were afraid. They'd screwed up, so they tried to hide and control God's perceptions about what happened. Hiding and controlling others amounts to nothing more than damage control. These responses do nothing to deal with the emotion of shame and our damaged sense of worth, but it is very often the best we can do when experiencing shame.

When I (Julie) was three years old, my grandmother was my primary caregiver. Her generation's parenting style involved massive doses of shame, fear, and control—such were the tools thought necessary to shape children into civilized and productive adults. I recall her sitting at the piano bench in the dining room as I faced her. She explained that I'd been naughty (although I have no idea what I did wrong) and then told me to bare my bottom, turn around, and bend over. After she spanked me, she walked away. No hug or comfort as I cried. No expression of love. She believed that consolation and affection would ruin a good spanking. At three years old, what I internalized and remembered from her discipline was not that my actions were wrong, but that I was wrong. She wanted to teach me about my behavior, but all I understood was that I was not lovable or worthy of respect.

Shame was reinforced many times in my young life, and I noticed and internalized every scrap of evidence that confirmed my suspicion that I was bad and unworthy of love. This process of self-verification is well documented in psychology. Simply stated, once you have an idea in your head about what you are like, you will tend to notice and accept information that confirms that idea and miss or reject information that disconfirms that idea. It's one reason we need to be transformed by the renewing of our minds (Romans 12:2). We need to allow God's love to change our self-perceptions. We need to stop seeing everything through lenses that confirm our deepest fears about ourselves—that we are wrong and worthless after all. This is why it is so vital for us to have God's perspective about us. Without it we will continue in a self-verification mode, looking for evidence that confirms what we already believe about ourselves (even when those beliefs are painful or negative).

I walked in shame for much of my life. I could not have verbalized the shame I felt or understood why I felt it. It was just an integral aspect of my existence. But early in my marriage, something happened that the Lord used to help identify my need for healing. A spirit of shame overplayed its hand that day, and I caught a glimpse of it. I can't say I got completely free that day, but I did see shame, for the first time, as something outside of myself that was tormenting me. It ran off before I got a good look—like sighting a fox at the forest's edge before it runs into the trees—but it was enough to start me on the journey of getting free.

That day I was in the kitchen, near the refrigerator. Having struggled with body-image and weight all my life, the refrigerator was a place I frequented a lot—often with a load of shame and self-hatred for being there. At that moment I wasn't even getting anything to eat. But when I heard my husband, Steve, open the bedroom door and start down the hallway, I jumped at the sound and quickly bolted into the adjacent sunroom. Fear of his judgment ("she's in the kitchen again") startled me into bolting to the sunroom to control his perception of me. With my heart racing, I realized just how ridiculous I had just been. My reaction to the sound of the door was over-the-top, and the Holy Spirit helped me see it for what it was: the spirit of shame. Although I am not a fan of "the devil made me do it" thinking, the truth in that moment was that nothing in the natural, not even the mild startle at hearing the door, accounted for the compulsive need to hide. What difference did it make if I was standing in the kitchen or the sunroom? None! The spirit of shame was tormenting me.

The best way to combat shame is to expose it rather than allowing it to hide. So I told Steve I'd jumped away from the refrigerator for no reason. I told him about the strong impulse to control his perceptions and to hide. My safe and wonderful husband prayed with me, and the enemy lost valuable ground that day. From then on, I began to see how much influence the spirit of shame had on my life. It was also the moment I realized that the devil tends to overplay his hand and push things a little too far. He's prideful and arrogant, but he's often not clever enough to know when to stop. Blinded by his pride and arrogance, he underestimates God's wisdom, love, and ability to reveal the truth to his kids. Since that day, I've seen the devil make this mistake time and time again. Disproportionate reactions are a strong clue that demonic activity is at work.

PRACTICAL APPLICATION

We encourage you to prayerfully consider the following signs and symptoms of shame. Ask the Holy Spirit to identify any specific area He wants to address right now to help you walk free.

Signs and Symptoms of Shame:

- Defensiveness; being overly sensitive to correction
- Difficulty admitting or accepting responsibility for mistakes
- Difficulty admitting problems
- Refusal/reluctance to admit wounds/hurt because it shows weakness
- Pride, arrogance, and/or self-righteousness
- Tendency to blame others for problems or mistakes
- A habit of justifying/rationalizing actions when confronted
- Refusal/reluctance to repent
- Tendency to shade the truth to avoid blame
- Tendency to tell lies/half-truths to self-protect
- A patronizing/condescending attitude toward others

- Tendency to make fun of others to make yourself feel better/superior
- Use of sarcasm
- Escaping/hiding
- Isolating
- Alienating others
- Independence/self-sufficiency
- Hidden envy/jealousy
- Tendency to compare yourself to others
- Perfectionism
- Self-sabotage (to avoid the shame of a failure for which we have no excuse)
- Self-punishment
- Anger/aggressive self-protection
- Unforgiving/bitter spirit
- Self-deprecation
- Passivity/lethargy/laziness (because shame often pushes you to perform perfectly until you get tired or burned out. Then you give up and give in to apathy and passivity. "Why bother?")

As you may discern from this list, shame, pride, and a punishing/unloving spirit often go together. Pride and a punishing/unloving spirit promise to protect our wounded heart. But this "protection" is just a demonic crust that prevents us from getting healed and being free to love and be loved without torment. It leads to hardness of heart because both pride and a punishing/unloving spirit deny the finished work of the cross. They leave you feeling unworthy to receive God's love, forgiveness, and healing. They tell you to punish yourself for being such a horrible person and then whisper that you're better than those who have hurt you.

If you see yourself in this list or know that shame has been influencing your responses to God and others, take heart. You can get free! Having identified the issue, you can do the work of admitting all over again your need for forgiveness. You can repent and renounce agreement with the spirit of shame. You have authority in the name of Jesus Christ to evict it. You can choose to receive the truth that God loves you. Exalt His name! Declare your freedom in Christ and ask for grace upon grace to walk in increasing victory.

Prayer to Break Agreement with a Spirit of Shame

Father, forgive me for partnering with a spirit of shame by so often choosing to hide from You and from other safe people in my life. Today I choose to come out of hiding and declare my faith and trust in Your love, goodness, kindness, and safety. I repent and renounce all agreement with a spirit of shame. I take back from that spirit all that is mine, washed in the blood of Jesus. Restore to me the joy of a loving relationship with You. I take back love, joy, peace, honor, respect, patience, and the expectation of good and not harm. Your word and Your promises to me are good. Your plans are to prosper and not harm me, to give me a hope and a future (Jeremiah 29:11). I break agreement with the lie that says I need to hide my shortcomings and failures from You. Cleanse my spirit, soul, and body of all deceit as I choose to acknowledge my sin and iniquity to You. Thank You for forgiving me the guilt of my sin (Psalm 32:1-5). Thank You for being patient with me in my failures. Teach me to walk in the light of Your love instead of the shadows of shame. In the name of Jesus Christ, I pray. Amen.

Rejection

Do not pay attention to every word that is spoken, or you may hear your servant cursing you (Ecclesiastes 7:21).

What then shall we say in response to these things? If God is for us, who can be against us (Romans 8:31)?

As with shame, everyone faces the sting of rejection. The job you hoped for went to someone else; you didn't get the part you practiced so hard for in the school play; the person you asked out turned you down, etc. Despite it being a common human experience, rejection can be like an arrow to the heart that can leave life-altering wounds if left unhealed. It can tempt you to believe lies about yourself (e.g., "I am not acceptable, loved, or valuable.") and lies about God (e.g., "He doesn't care about me. He's good to other people, but not to me."). When we hear these kinds of thoughts and agree with them, which is easy to do after a rejection, we fall into the enemy's trap. We have discussed how the enemy convinced Eve to believe the lie that God is not fully good. Rejection sells the same lie in different packaging. "How could God be good when I feel SO bad right now, when people don't like me or value me?" If we believe the lie long enough, we come to see ourselves as truly unworthy to be loved, and we even begin to reject ourselves.

Consider the following facts about rejection:[22]

1. Rejection shares the same neural pathways in the brain as physical pain, which is why rejection literally hurts!

2. Physical pain relievers like acetaminophen (aka, Tylenol) can alleviate the emotional pain of rejection just as it alleviates physical pain.

3. We more easily remember and re-experience the pain of rejection than physical pain.

4. Rejection threatens our sense of belonging and connection. If we can affirm our belonging after being rejected, we will feel better. If not, we will feel lonely and angry.

5. Anger is a very common response to rejection. Studies have even shown a link between rejection and the risk of adolescent violence, even greater than the link between violence and drugs, poverty, or gang membership!

6. Rejection often turns inward. After a rejection, we will very often blame ourselves and focus on everything that is wrong with us rather than being able to see the situation objectively.

7. The pain of rejection temporarily affects our ability to think clearly, remember, and make decisions.

8. Rejection causes emotional pain. We cannot "reason" our way out of hurt feelings because reason does not soothe emotional pain. Telling ourselves not to feel bad doesn't help. Having others tell us we shouldn't feel bad doesn't help, either. Even knowing that the basis of the rejection was false does nothing to alleviate the pain once it has been triggered.

The pain of rejection can lead to a variety of ungodly responses. As you read the following list, we encourage you to ask the Holy Spirit to highlight anything He wants to help you address.

---

22 https://www.psychologytoday.com/us/blog/the-squeaky-wheel/201307/10-surprising-facts-about-rejection

Ungodly responses to rejection:

- Abandonment/Fear of abandonment
- Adultery/Fornication
- Anger/Rage
- Argument escalation
- Codependency
- Complaining/Critical spirit/Fault-Finding
- Depression/Despair
- Discontent
- Doubt
- Drivenness
- Envy/Jealousy
- False burden bearing
- False responsibility
- Frustration of feeling misunderstood
- Guilt
- Hatred
- Hyper need for acceptance or approval
- Hyper need for identity
- Hyper need to be loved
- Idolatry
- Ingratitude/Lack of thankfulness
- Insecurity
- Isolation
- Legalism
- Loneliness
- Low self-esteem
- Lust
- Lying
- Manipulation
- Occult involvement
- Perceived rejection
- Perfectionism
- Preemptive rejection (rejecting others first)
- Quick to feel slighted/Easily offended
- Rebellion
- Resentment
- Retaliation
- Self-pity
- Self-protection
- Self-rejection

- Shame
- Stubbornness
- Unbelief
- Unforgiveness
- Victimization
- Violence

God created us with an innate need to belong, to be loved and accept-ed. Rejection is one of the most devastating things a human heart can experi-ence because it is the polar opposite of what the Father created us for. The experience of rejection opens the door to doubt and unbelief in our hearts. God's word says we are accepted by Him through His son Jesus. He's already adopted us into His family (Ephesians 1:5). But rejection tells us we must be accepted by people. If we care more about the acceptance of others, we get blinded to the love of the Father. Valuing and seeking human love and approval more than the love of God is idolatry.

The spirit of rejection is the idol, the little household god that makes demands we can never fully satisfy. It is a harsh taskmaster, impossible to please. Despite our best efforts and the sacrifices we make to it, the spirit of rejection will prevent us from truly feeling accepted and loved. Every ambiguous interaction will be perceived as rejection. It torments us with insecurity and gets us to second-guess every look, every phrase, every text message, every delayed response to a text, every teasing remark, every question, every request, every invitation we didn't get. Once rejection has taken root in our hearts and minds, we don't even have to be truly rejected to feel its sting. We expect it, so we see everything through the filter of that expectation. The taskmaster is never satisfied to let you rest in the knowledge that you're okay, that you're loved.

In cases of true rejection, a natural response is anger. Rejection blocks the goal of connection. Another natural response is sadness because the rejection makes it impossible to connect in the way we desired. But these emotions can become fodder for demonic torment if we do not process them honestly (see Module 4 for more on emotions). For example, the initial anger of be-ing rejected can lead to ruminating over the unfairness of the rejection. And that can lead to bitterness. Unchecked, bitterness leads to the fruit of criti-cism, sarcasm, resentment, and even retaliation. The rejected learn to reject others first and in spades. That is, we learn to do it preemptively. We reject first and forcefully before we feel the sting of rejection again for ourselves. When battling a spirit of rejection, we typically need to address an unloving spirit, anger, bitterness, and unforgiveness for full healing and freedom to come. The good news is that His love, acceptance, and power can overcome rejection and all its repercussions. He is well able to set us free spirit, soul, and body! When we know who we are and Whose we are, when we understand that we are fully accepted and loved by our heavenly Father, this breaks the power of the lie that we are rejected. We are transformed as we renew our minds by meditating on His word and allowing His love to soothe our hurting hearts. It changes things! His banner over us is love (Song of Solomon 2:4)!

See what great love the Father has lavished on us, that we should be called children of God! And that is what we are (1 John 3:1, NIV)!

The LORD appeared to us in the past, saying: "I have loved you with an everlasting love; I have drawn you with loving devotion" (Jeremiah 31:3).

By this we know what love is: Jesus laid down His life for us, and we ought to lay down our lives for our brothers (1 John 3:16).

There is no greater love than to lay down one's life for one's friends (John 15:13, NLT).

Above all, love one another deeply, because love covers over a multitude of sins (1 Peter 4:8).

But God proves His love for us in this: While we were still sinners, Christ died for us (Romans 5:8).

I will declare that your love stands firm forever, that you have established your faithfulness in heaven itself (Psalm 89:2, NIV).

Prayer and Declaration Against Rejection

In the name of Jesus Christ, I declare that the spirit of rejection is a liar who has falsely accused me of being unloved and unlovable. I reject this false identity and choose to receive and accept His love for me. He says that I am loved and accepted—and so I am! I choose to agree with His word. I agree with what He agrees with and love what He loves, so I can say, believe, and know in my heart and mind that I am fully loved. I choose to follow Him in His love for me. I choose not to reject myself because He never rejects me. I choose to forgive and love myself as He does. I choose to love and forgive others as I follow Him. Father, in the name of Jesus

Christ, I choose this day to renounce and repent of agreeing with any spirit of rejection. I take responsibility for past agreements and ask You to break the power of rejection in my life and through my generations. I ask Your forgiveness for agreeing with what is so contrary to Your heart. Thank You for revealing truth, and thank You for forgiving me. Having rejected the spirit of rejection, I tell it to go now in the name of Jesus! Help me, Father God, to walk in newness of life. Change me from glory to glory, and fill me with Your presence. I ask for revelation of Your love and acceptance for me so I can walk in healing and bring Your love to those around me in Jesus' name. Thank You, Father, for loving and healing me! Amen.

Fear

The dictionary[23] defines fear as "a distressing emotion aroused by impending danger, evil, pain, etc., whether the threat is real or imagined; the feeling or condition of being afraid." Healthy fear (our fight, flight, or freeze reaction) stimulates us to take action to get out of the way of danger. Once the danger is gone, the fear should go, too. Fear becomes a problem when it persists beyond a dangerous situation and pervades our thinking continually. Fight or flight processes in the brain are meant to be short and temporary bursts that shut down areas of our brains so that other areas can take precedence in getting us to safety. But this reaction is not meant to last (see Module 4). Fear is unhealthy when it does not dissipate after the danger is gone. Unhealthy fear can create feelings of paralysis, shame, and irrational thinking. To be sure, fear plays an important part in our survival when we are faced with life-or-death situations. Growing up in California, we were taught it's wise to have things like extra canned goods, water, and other necessities to hold our families over for a few days in the case of supply chain delays and/or power outages due to fires or earthquakes. Storms and natural disasters happen, so being prepared is wise. It's good to be cautious, right? It's wise to be prepared and in control, right? Yes, except when it's not. Fear disguises itself. Disguise is a favorite way the enemy infects our lives with fear and other torments (2 Corinthians 11:14). When we allow unhealthy fear to scream in the background ... well, Houston, we have a problem.

The dictionary definition of wisdom is "the quality or state of being wise; knowledge of what is true or right coupled with just judgment as to action ...discernment, or insight." We need to be aware that a spirit of fear will often disguise itself as "wisdom." I (Sally) first became aware of this fact when a woman at my church prophesied one night at a special prayer service. She said,

---

23 www.dictionary.com

"Beware the fear disguised as wisdom." Her words really struck me because they helped me realize how much I had been battling fear in the days leading up to the prayer event. Up until the moment I heard those words, I hadn't even realized I was in a battle. But for sure, the enemy didn't want me at that service. He didn't want me to get free. He wanted me tormented without me knowing it.

We can also be socialized to experience unhealthy fear and think it's normal. For example, we may have learned to think of God as a scary Santa Claus in the sky, keeping track of whether we are "naughty or nice." A God who withholds blessings if we are "bad" instead of "good, for goodness' sake!" This kind of "Santa Claus fear" creates shame and doubt, causing us to expect disapproval and avoid being in His presence. It leads us to expect divine punishment even if we know in our heads that we are loved and forgiven. It can cause us to misinterpret verses like Matthew 5:48 (NIV) through a distorted lens: *Be perfect, therefore, as your heavenly Father is perfect.* "Perfect" in this verse doesn't mean mistake-free or "nice" rather than "naughty." It means to be whole and complete, to have reached the full extent of one's purpose, having completed the process. It means to be full-grown and mature, lacking nothing.[24] This verse is saying "be whole, complete, mature, and purposeful as your heavenly Father is whole, complete, mature, and purposeful."

There is no fear in love [dread does not exist]. But perfect (complete, full-grown) love drives out fear, because fear involves [the expectation of divine] punishment, so the one who is afraid [of God's judgment] is not perfected in love [has not grown into a sufficient understanding of God's love] (1 John 4:18, AMP).

This important verse teaches us that whole, complete, mature love casts out fear, including the fear of punishment. So the more we allow the Holy Spirit to grow us up in love, the more fear must go! As we become increasingly able to receive His perfect love, the less room there is for unhealthy fear and anxiety. The less room there is for Santa Claus fear of punishment. We become progressively more able to walk in freedom and grow in wisdom.

How can we know what is unhealthy fear and what is true wisdom? I (Sally) had a teacher in Bible College who would say the Bible is a "guardrail that keeps us from going off track in life." It is incredibly easy for the human heart to be overtaken by fear, but God's word has much wisdom to say about fear and how we don't have to be afraid. It teaches us that God is with us and helps us overcome our fear. As we have seen, God's perfect love casts out fear. In a different translation, the rest of the verse says that

---

24 www.biblehub.com

fear involves torment (1 John 4:18, NKJV). Using this scripture as a guardrail, we have a big clue as to the difference between fear and wisdom: If our mind is tormented by a particular fear, that fear is not wisdom!

We fight spiritual battles against fear (or anything else) by putting the word of God into action, as we see in these verses:

For God did not give us a spirit of timidity or cowardice or fear, but [He has given us a spirit] of power and of love and of sound judgment and personal discipline [abilities that result in a calm, well-balanced mind and self-control] (2 Timothy 1:7, AMP).

If any of you lacks wisdom [to guide him through a decision or circumstance], he is to ask of [our benevolent] God, who gives to everyone generously and without rebuke or blame, and it will be given to him (James 1:5, AMP).

He who trusts confidently in his own heart is a [dull, thickheaded] fool, but he who walks in [skillful and godly] wisdom will be rescued (Proverbs 28:26, AMP).

Get [skillful and godly] wisdom! Acquire understanding [actively seek spiritual discernment, mature comprehension, and logical interpretation]! Do not forget nor turn away from the words of my mouth. Do not turn away from her (Wisdom) and she will guard and protect you; Love her, and she will watch over you (Proverbs 4:5-6, AMP).

The beginning of wisdom is found in aligning our spirit, soul, and body with the truth of scripture. We partner with God to cast out fear when we actively seek His loving presence because where love is lacking, fear is lurking. So, we overcome a spirit of fear by being filled to overflowing with the perfect love of God. As we choose to worship Him, regarding Him as truly awesome (awe, not terror, is what the "fear of the Lord" is all about), our love for Him grows and the fear goes. In addition, as we are progressively "perfected" (made whole and complete) in love, leaning on the Lord (Proverbs 3:5-6), we also mature in spiritual wisdom and discernment.

Prayer for Wisdom and Freedom from Fear of Punishment

Father, I thank You that through the cross of Your Son Jesus Christ, I have been set free from the law of sin and death. I repent for and renounce agreement with the lie that I deserve punishment and that You are keeping track of my sins like Santa Claus. I thank You, Jesus, that You bore my sin and shame on the cross and suffered my punishment to set me free. You said, "It is finished," and I believe You. From this day forward, I declare that I will no longer partner with fear and its lies. Thank You for forgiveness, grace, and perfect love. Thank You that Your amazing love casts fear far from me. I open my heart to You and ask You to fill me with Your perfect love. Fill me with awe and wonder, with wisdom and understanding, with spiritual insight and discernment. I desire to be "whole and complete" as You are "whole and complete." In the name of Jesus Christ, I pray. Amen.

Faith Over Fear: Can I really let go?

For God has not given us a spirit of fear, but of power and of love and of a sound mind (2 Timothy 1:7, NKJV).

Many years ago, I (Sally) had a dream that I was floating in an ocean surrounded by many other people. We were all clinging for dear life to massive hanging ropes, but the ropes were just floating from the sky not anchored to anything. One by one, people began to let go of their ropes. They were floating and laughing in complete abandon. All the fear they had shown while clinging to their rope was gone and the rope was gone, too. As I watched, more and more people let go as fears gave way to freedom. I wanted to let go, too, but I just couldn't seem to bring myself to release my grip on the rope. When I woke up, I asked the Lord what the dream meant. I felt Him say, "See, Sally, when you are clinging to the wrong thing, there is fear and doubt. If you would just let go, you would see that I've got you." I was clinging to what I thought brought me security. But I saw that true freedom, security, and joy was in letting go and believing that the Father is worthy of my trust. His freedom is real and tangible. Choosing faith over fear is imperative.

Scripture gives us many examples of people who went through incredibly dangerous and scary situations. We can see how their choice of faith or fear worked out for them. Faith is trust. Fear is faith (trust) in the wrong kingdom. I think of faith as being like currency. We decide how to spend or invest, which then determines our return. If I put my faith and trust in God, my return is peace—even in the middle of hard or dangerous situations (such as Daniel in the lion's den; Daniel 6). If I invest in fear by agreeing with it and trusting it, then my "return" is torment, anxiety, and a lack of peace (such as King Saul; 1 Samuel 10:22, 13:11-14, 15:24-26, 16:14). Fear would love us to stay stuck in cycles of self-doubt and the inability to move forward (such as the Israelites on the edge of the Promised Land; Numbers 13-14). Fear would love us to think we will always be stuck clinging to a rope over a watery abyss.

But we do not have to stay stuck in fear and torment. I love the story of Gideon (Judges 6). It is an incredible story of how God helped him overcome fear and defeat the enemy. As one who has struggled with fear, often crippling fear, for much of my life, Gideon's story brings me so much hope. There can be so much shame and guilt attached to fear. We feel fear, then we beat ourselves up for feeling it! We tell ourselves we should have more faith, or we should be able to "get over it." Sometimes we feel like God is mad at us for being so weak. I have felt all these things, but then I read about Gideon.

An angel appears to Gideon as he is beating wheat in a winepress (Judges 6:11). He was hiding from the Midianites who had been oppressing the Israelites for seven years. Every harvest, they would come and take everything. Gideon was hiding in hopes of saving enough food to stay alive. It's here, while he is hiding from his enemy, that the angel says, *The Lord is with you, you mighty man of [fearless] courage* (Judges 6:12, AMPC). Um, what? Mighty? Fearless? Gideon's response is not that of someone who sees himself as a "mighty man of fearless courage." Nor is it a response of faith. He basically says, "Where's this amazing God we were told about? He's forsaken us." The Lord then tells him how he, Gideon, will be the one who will deliver his people from their enemy. Gideon's next response is from a "worm's eye" view: "My clan is the poorest, and I am the least in my father's house." The rest of the chapter and the next two chapters detail how God addresses and helps Gideon overcome his doubts. He shows Gideon that he truly is who God says he is, able to do all the things set before him in the Lord's strength. God doesn't shame him, condemn him, or beat him up for his fear. He simply speaks identity and purpose over him in the middle of his fear and brings him through to fulfill that purpose. Gideon's part was to be obedient despite his fear, and the Lord brought victory over his enemy and peace to the land. In fact, Gideon built an altar to the Lord and called it "The Lord is Peace" (Judges 6:24). Yes! Gideon, the guy hiding in a winepress at the beginning of the story, has been transformed by a loving God into a victorious, mighty man of fearless courage and peace!

The example of Gideon shows us that we can trust and obey even amid challenging and fearful situations. Similarly, the example of David when he confronted the giant Goliath shows us that faith can bring victory even against overwhelming odds. David encouraged himself in the Lord, reminding himself of previous dangerous situations he had faced. God had given him victory over lions and bears, and he expected God to give him victory over Goliath and all the Philistines (1 Samuel 17). He had history with God, and he found courage in recalling God's faithfulness in those previous situations.

But we don't have to have overcome lions and bears to stand in faith over fear. Look at how King Jehoshaphat responded when he was told a huge army had gathered against the kingdom of Judah.

Jehoshaphat was terrified by this news and begged the Lord for guidance. He also ordered everyone in Judah to begin fasting. So people from all the towns of Judah came to Jerusalem to seek the Lord's help (2 Chronicles 20:3-4).

Jehoshaphat had good reason to be terrified. He could not possibly have withstood the force of the three armies set against him. But he does not continue in his fear or react faithlessly because of it. Instead, he prays and calls on his people to pray and fast, too. His prayer (2 Chronicles 20:6-12) is all about how God had taken care of His people in the past, about the amazing things He had done—things Jehoshaphat had not seen personally. Yet he stood in faith, remembering what God had done for others, encouraged through experiences he had only heard of. King Jehoshaphat and all of Judah prayed and worshiped when facing overwhelming odds, and then God gave them an unusual battle plan: don't fight (vs. 17)! The next day, the singers went out before the army singing, *Give thanks to the Lord. His faithful love endures forever* (vs. 21, NLT)! The moment they started singing, God moved on their behalf (vs. 22), and the opposing army became confused and destroyed themselves!

King David and King Jehoshaphat show us what we can do when fear tries to overwhelm us: We can remind ourselves of the great things God has done. If we have a history of seeing God deliver us, we remind ourselves of those times and find strength and encouragement to face this new challenge. But even if we don't yet have those personal victories, we can find encouragement in the victories God has given others. His love and faithfulness never change, and what He can do for one He can do for all!

PRACTICAL APPLICATION

The Bible has a lot to say about fear, most often encouraging us not to be afraid because fear is "faith" in the wrong kingdom. Still, we all battle it to some degree or another. If fear is a big problem for you, here are some points to ponder. Consider writing these scriptures in your journal and memorizing one or more of them:

- Fear is torment (1 John 4:18)
- Fear steals our peace (Philippians 4:6-7)
- Fear can be an evil spirit (2 Timothy 1:7)
- Fear tries to magnify the enemy's power to appear bigger than it is (Is. 54:17)
- Fear inhibits our ability to trust God (Proverbs 3:5-6)
- Fear tempts us to give up (Is. 41:10)
- Fear tries to separate us from God (Romans 8:38-39)
- God frees us from our fear when we cry out to Him (Psalm 34:4)

We also encourage you to read and pray over the following list. Ask God to show you any areas of struggle. The list is meant to help identify fears that may be hidden, but it is in no way exhaustive. The Lord may identify areas of fear that are not listed here.

- Fear of illness/disease
- Fear of death
- Fear of death of loved ones
- Fear of abandonment
- Fear of failure
- Fear of rejection
- Fear of man
- Fear of pain
- Fear of doctors/dentists/medical procedures
- Fear of poverty/lack
- Fear of success
- Fear of change
- Fear of the future/unknown
- Fear of God's judgment/legalism

- Fear of losing salvation
- Fear of being alone
- Fear of losing control
- Fear of embarrassment
- Fear of anger/violence in others
- Fear of manipulation
- Fear of dependency on others
- Fear of superstition
- Fear of dreams
- Fear of conflict
- Fear of accidents
- Fear of family members
- Fear of intimacy
- Fear of inadequacy
- Fear of shame

Finally, pray over every area of fear and struggle that the Lord has shown you. You may want to use the following prayer as a guide to disagreeing with the enemy and evicting any and all fear spirits. Follow up by exalting the Lord and declaring the truths of his word!

Prayer to Break Agreement with Fear

Father, in the name of Jesus Christ, I choose this day to renounce and repent for agreeing with the fear of_____. I take responsibility and ask You to break the power of this fear in my life and through my generations. I ask for Your forgiveness for agreeing with what is so contrary to Your heart, and I receive Your forgiveness in Jesus' name. Thank You for revealing truth and thank You for forgiving me. I choose not to partner or agree with a spirit of fear—it is no longer welcome, and I tell it to go in Jesus' name! Help me walk in newness of life. Change me from glory to glory. Fill me with Your presence. Thank You, Father, for loving and setting me free! Amen.

MODULE 4

LEGALLY FREE

Therefore, my beloved, just as you have always obeyed, not only in my presence, but now even more in my absence, continue to work out your salvation with fear and trembling. For it is God who works in you to will and to act on behalf of His good purpose (Philippians 2:12-13).

Whatever you have learned or received or heard from me, or seen in me, put it into practice. And the God of peace will be with you (Philippians 4:9).

In this module, we focus on living free in our deeds, the things we do. Despite contention from satan and despite our own fear and doubt, we are truly and legally free to walk out freedom in practical ways. We emphasize perseverance over perfection because we live in an age between the resurrection and Christ's return. Our freedom from sin, satan, and self will be complete—whole, perfect, and without challenge—only when Christ returns to deal the final blow to satan's kingdom. Until then, let's encourage one another to live up to what we've already attained and to press on for more (Philippians 3:12-16).

As you will see, the main topics covered in this module are organized in terms of our acronym, **INDEED**: **I**dentify, **N**eed, **D**isagree, **E**vict, **E**xalt, and **D**eclare.

Identify: Am I living free or just managing?

The Christian faith is largely characterized by paradox—tension between two truths that appear to be contradictory. For example, to keep our lives, we must lose them (Matthew 16:25); when we are weak, then we are strong (2 Corinthians 12:10); to be the greatest, we must be the least (Mark 10:43-44). You get the idea. As we continue to walk out our freedom in Christ, we must grapple with the paradox of "the now and the not yet." It is true that we are free indeed, but our freedom is not yet entirely evident. We are seated with Christ in the heavenly places (Ephesians 2:6), but our daily experience is in the natural world with our boots on the ground. In the following passage, Paul declares that we are sons not slaves. We are free now to receive our inheritance as co-heirs with Christ (Romans 8:17). Yet we often behave like slaves because we are not mature:

I mean that the heir, as long as he is a child, is no different from a slave, though he is the owner of everything, but he is under guardians and managers until the date set by his father. In the same way we also, when we were children, were enslaved to the elementary principles of the world. But when the fullness of time had come, God sent forth his Son, born of woman, born under the law, to redeem those who were under the law, so that we might receive adoption as sons. And because you are sons, God has sent the Spirit of his Son into our hearts, crying, "Abba! Father!" So you are no longer a slave, but a son, and if a son, then an heir through God (Galatians 4:1-7, ESV).

Children need a guardian to look after them and help them, and the Holy Spirit was sent to help us in our weakness (Romans 8:26). There is no shame in acknowledging our immaturity. But just managing our issues is not the same thing as freedom. We are called to grow up in our salvation (1 Peter 2:2), to grow up into Christ Himself (Ephesians 4:15). Thankfully, we can invite the Holy Spirit to search our hearts and identify our places of immaturity, any way in which we're still behaving like slaves. He will lovingly reveal those areas where we are still just trying to manage. Remember, it is the Father's joy and delight to sanctify us in the bubble bath of His kindness and mercy.

If you have died with Christ to the spiritual forces of the world, why, as though you still belonged to the world, do you submit to its regulations: "Do not handle, do not taste, do not touch!"? These will all perish with use, because they are based on human commands and teachings. Such restrictions indeed have an appearance of wisdom, with their self-prescribed worship, their false humility, and their harsh treatment of the body; but they are of no value against the indulgence of the flesh (Colossians 2:20-23).

What does have real value against the temptations of the world, the flesh, and the devil is a deep and loving connection with the Father. We can rest in the assurance that we are dearly loved sons and daughters. We can relinquish self-management and self-effort and live in the light of His goodness. We can live free of guilt and condemnation because we are already fully pardoned. Granted amnesty. When we relinquish the right to do it ourselves, we receive the Holy Spirit's help to grow, change, or amend whatever needs amending. When we are weak, then we are strong and fully empowered to choose what pleases the Lord over what indulges our flesh. We can bring the "not yet" closer and closer to the "now."

Prayer of Relinquishment

Holy Spirit, thank You for speaking assurance to my heart that I am a child of God. I am no longer a slave. Help me to grow up and receive my full inheritance in You. I renounce and relinquish self-management and ask You to take that role in my life. I acknowledge that managing demons and temptations is not the same thing as being free. I want true, legal, and practical freedom from everything that hinders me from living an abundantly fruitful life in Your kingdom. Thank You for giving me a home in Your family. Thank You for throwing me a lifeline of love. Draw me closer and closer with Your "cords of kindness and ropes of love" (Hosea 11:4). In the name of Jesus Christ, I pray. Amen.

Need: What's up with my emotions, and why can't I just move on?

Emotions are a good gift from God. They are an expression of His nature and part of what it means to be created in His image. God has intense emotions! Throughout scripture we see evidence of His delight, passion, longing, anger, sadness, grief, and more. (We do not see Him expressing fear, of course, because God is love and there is no fear in love.) It is freeing to see how passionate and emotional God truly is. Throughout scripture He shares His heart with us and expresses His passion without ever compromising His holiness. Amazing!

Obviously, we are not yet perfect as He is perfect. We need the Lord to help us deal honestly with our emotions because a healthy emotional life can make living free in deed (action) so much easier. We can't just "move on" without dealing honestly with our pain, anger, grief, etc., because unprocessed emotions can be an open door to the enemy. Thus, the better we get at dealing with our emotions, the less access the enemy has to harass and torment us (see Ephesians 4:26-27; 2 Corinthians 2:10-11; Hebrews 12:14-15).

Much of our difficulty with emotion is rooted in aversive childhood experiences. Many of us see through lenses ("perspectives") created by traumas that become triggers. The enemy is quick to barge into an open emotional door and offer "benefits" and strategies for dealing with confusing or painful situations. We need the Lord to help us identify those self-protective strategies—such as self-comfort, self-reliance, revenge, numbness, apathy, sarcasm, and so on. These may have helped us cope and survive in the moment, but with repeated use, they become ungodly soul habits that leave us emotionally isolated and/or weak. The emotional fortress that such strategies create may have kept us safe initially, but now it leaves us stuck in solitary confinement and prisoners to pain. It doesn't have to be this way. With a little knowledge, time, and effort we can learn to respond to emotions intelligently and intentionally, processing them appropriately rather than reacting to triggers automatically. We can break free from the cycle of pain (see page 144) and walk out of our self-imposed prison.

Recall from Module 1 that we have a triune nature—spirit, soul, and body. Our spirits, aligned with Holy spirit, need to be in charge so that we do not lead with our head or our heart. Most of us have a lot of work to do! Some of us live primarily in our heads, from a place of reason and logic. Others live primarily from our hearts, emoting first and thinking later (if at all). All of us can grow in understanding more about how to process and express emotions in healthy ways. We don't have to deny/avoid our emotions, on the one hand, or hyperfocus on them, on the other. We need the Lord to sanctify our emotions—to set them apart for their intended use—and teach us how to better experience and express them as He intended.

Especially if you are a "head" person, you may need to hear that emotions are valid, God-given responses to events and circumstances. Though emotional responses may not represent the lasting "Truth" about a situation, they are nevertheless true experiences. Emotions should not be discounted or scorned in ourselves or others. God cares about our emotional life. He weeps and rejoices with us, and He calls us to do the same for others (Romans 12:15). Sometimes "head" people can be so focused on truth that they forget to speak it in love (Ephesians 4:15), which ends up adding to a person's hurt rather than solving anything. Truth without love or a willingness to connect with another person's heart, is just hurtful noise (1 Corinthians 13:1). And "heart" people may need to hear that you do not have to let your emotions take over or tyrannize your choices or how you respond to others. The point here is that we all have some growing up to do when it comes to dealing well with our own and others' strong emotions. We need Jesus!

Not many of us have had any explicit teaching on what emotions are, what usually triggers them, what they are for, or how to clue in to what they are telling us. This lack of understanding handicaps our ability to deal effectively with our own and others' emotions. In the following paragraphs, I (Julie) elaborate on four important truths about emotions: (1) They are morally neutral. (2) They are temporary. (3) They need to be acknowledged and named rather than avoided. (4) They provide useful, often actionable, information.

First, emotions are morally neutral. The enemy has twisted our perceptions and convinced many Christians that negative emotions such as anger or disgust are wrong to feel. Not true! Emotions are reflexive, involuntary responses (like blinking or startling at an unexpected noise). They are part of our good, God-given nature. It is what we do with our emotions that can be good or bad. It is good when they draw us toward God and others (2 Corinthians 7:10; Psalm 42 and 43; Proverbs 17:17). It is not good when we respond to intense emotions by isolating ourselves (Proverbs 18:1), ruminating on negative things (Philippians 4:8), or rehearsing rather than resolving our issues (1 Corinthians 13:5; Ephesians 4:26-27).

Second, intense emotions are temporary. Many people feel like strong emotions will kill them. But emotions get spent quickly. Though they can be uncomfortable to feel and to witness in others, strong emotional reactions will pass. A common tactic of the enemy is to convince us that emotions are too powerful and overwhelming to face. He convinces us that if we were to let ourselves feel their full force, we would be incapacitated somehow. We can combat this lie with the truth that emotions are, by definition, intense but short-lived. If a feeling lingers for hours or days, it is no longer an emotion but has become a mood and/or a mindset.

I think of strong emotions as ocean waves. When we appreciate their transience, we can be less afraid of their intensity and less inclined to avoid them. Take grief as an example. In the early stages, the intense pain of loss may feel like a tsunami that will kill us. It won't. Though the waves are fast, furious, and frequent, they always recede. Allowing ourselves to feel the grief as it washes over us is healthy, even if it feels like we will drown. When we let the waves wash over us, our soul and body will process the loss more effectively than if we stuff the pain or numb ourselves to it. What's so bad about avoiding negative emotions? For one, it's not physically healthy to suppress our emotions. When we don't process them honestly—naming and acknowledging what triggered them—their residue lingers. Our bodies can get stuck in a stress-response that can have serious long-term consequences for both physical and mental health.[25] For another, it's not spiritually healthy to avoid our emotions or pretend they don't affect us. As already mentioned, our emotional dishonesty and/or self-reliance opens a door for the enemy to build strongholds in our lives.

Third, emotions need to be acknowledged and named rather than avoided. It may seem counterintuitive, but when we name our emotions (or the emotion we see in others) it helps our mind and body process appropriately rather than getting stuck. Let me briefly describe the research evidence that supports this claim. In one study, people saw faces expressing anger, fear, happiness, or surprise. Brain imaging (fMRI) data were collected while the participants responded to the images by either choosing the label that matched the emotion they were seeing, choosing another face with a matching emotion, or choosing another face with a matching gender. Those who labeled the emotions showed reduced activity in the emotional processing center of the brain (the amygdala). In other words, naming the emotion helped the brain process it and let it go. One might think that naming an emotion would amplify its impact, but just the opposite was observed.[26] Another study showed that individuals who owned and articulated their fear of spiders were less fearful of them a week later (as measured by their physiological responses) compared to those who were instructed to claim that the spider didn't bother them and compared to others who were told to distract themselves by thinking of something other than the spider. So, owning and naming the fear resulted in better coping a week later than either lying to or distracting oneself![27] What we can learn from this work is that if we face our fear or anger or whatever and own it for what it is, we will be able to process it and release it faster than if we do not. Emotional honesty is a superpower!

Fourth, emotions provide useful, often actionable, information, and we need to learn to pay attention to what emotions are designed to tell us. When we

25 Van der Kolk, B. (2014). The Body Keeps the Score: Brain, Mind, and Body in the Healing of Trauma. Viking.

26 Lieberman, M. D., Eisenberger, N. I., Crockett, M. J., Tom, S. M., Pfeifer, J. H., & Way, B. M. (2007). Putting feelings into words: Affect labeling disrupts amygdala activity in response to affective stimuli. Psychological Science, 18(5), 421-428.

27 Kircanski, K., Lieberman, M. D., & Craske, M. G. (2012). Feelings into words: Contributions of language to exposure therapy. Psychological Science, 23(10), 1086-1091.

understand what triggers an emotion and what purpose it is supposed to serve, we can more easily name it (see the previous point). We can more easily let it go when it is spent (point number two). And we can more easily cooperate with that emotion's God-given purpose rather than be drawn into sin (point number one).

In his book *Victory Over Darkness*, Neil Anderson teaches that **anger** is typically triggered by a blocked goal. It is also triggered by perceived injustice (because most of us have the implicit goal of being treated fairly). Thus, if we are experiencing intense anger, we can choose to take a step back, evaluate what goal is being blocked, and consider whether we need to remove the obstacle or change the goal. Either way, evaluating the situation gives us something to focus on and name rather than continuing to act in blind rage. When anger is the result of perceived injustice, we can take it to the Lord and partner with him to right the wrong (Micah 6:8). Next, according to Anderson, **anxiety** is the result of an uncertain goal. For example, if we are interested in asking someone out on a date but we aren't certain of the response we'll get, we will be feeling anxious. In general, when we experience anxiety we need to look for what uncertainties are bothering us. We can then talk to the Lord about these things and choose to trust the outcomes to Him. When we do that, His peace guards our hearts and sets us free from fear (Philippians 4:6-7). Finally, Anderson says that **depression** signals an impossible goal. For example, the grief of losing a loved one can lead us into depression when we stay in denial about the loss and/ or focus on the intense desire to have the person with us still. (This might look like keeping the loved one's room exactly as it was when they died.) The impossible goal may not be obvious to ourselves or others. But we may be inadvertently pursuing an impossible goal when we do things like base our sense of worth on how others treat us or when we try to get others to do what we think is right. These are impossible goals that may well lead us into depression because we cannot control what other people think or do.

Below is a list of five more negative emotions along with their typical triggers and the purpose they serve.[28]

- **Sadness** is triggered by unwanted separation, loss, or failure to obtain a goal. It motivates us to reverse, repair, or replace the separation, failure, or loss. As already mentioned, pursuing impossible goals (such as making someone change—impossible because we do not control their choices) can trigger sadness that can lead to depression and hopelessness.

---

28 Reeve, J. (2018). *Understanding Motivation and Emotion*, 7th ed. Wiley.

- **Fear** is triggered by a perceived threat or danger. (We are not talking about irrational fear or a demonic spirit of fear.) The purpose of fear is protection. It motivates us to avoid the threat, flee from it, or fight it. As Christians, the best response to fear is to run to God immediately. He alone is our protection (Psalm 91).
- **Disgust** is triggered by something spoiled or repulsive. Disgust motivates us to get away from the spoiled object. At a basic level, disgust helps us survive and stay well.
- **Guilt** is triggered by mistakes and failure. The purpose of guilt is to move us to make amends and to change or improve our behavior. It moves us to repair a broken connection with someone.
- **Shame** is triggered by a sense of failure or inadequacy to live up to an ideal. In its healthiest form, shame motivates us to restore a sense of personal worth and adequacy in the context of safe relationships and connection. In its unhealthy and most common form, shame motivates disconnection, hiding, isolation, and self-protection.

Knowing the triggers and basic function of each emotion is a good starting point for improving our emotional coping skills. Still, there will be times when the next right step is not immediately apparent. At such times, we can ask the Holy Spirit to help us work through what we're feeling, why we're feeling that way, and what we can do about it. When we invite Him into those moments, He shows up without fail (whether we feel Him or not). When we ask for help and wisdom, He provides and guides. He may show us an action step we haven't yet considered, or He may just offer the comfort of His presence in the situation. Either way, naming and facing the emotion honestly and directly is the best way to deal with it.

PRACTICAL APPLICATION

Learning to deal well with emotions is not a one-and-done proposition. Many of us have a lifetime of bad emotional habits to overcome. A common tendency is to consider emotions a weakness, and so we often ignore and suppress them rather than face and feel them. If that describes you, please be patient with yourself. We encourage you to be willing to face the wave, pursue emotional courage, and persevere as you develop new emotional habits.

You could begin by prayerfully considering the common negative emotions we discussed. As you consider your typical responses to these emotions, ask the Holy Spirit to show you any ungodly coping mechanisms or habits you have developed to deal with one or more of them. Then ask Him to help you learn to respond in a healthier, more godly way whenever that emotion gets triggered. It can be extremely helpful to have a friend in whom you can confide and who can help you through emotional challenges as they arise.

It is also helpful to pray for wisdom to discern whether your emotion is a legitimate response to the trigger or whether it is out of proportion in the specific situation. Typically, an over-the-top emotional response means there is unresolved pain amplifying the response. Such amplification is a clue that deeper work is required to experience emotional health and freedom. Often, unforgiveness is an issue. If you continue to ignore the pain or the possibility that you may need to forgive (even if that means forgiving yourself), then the enemy may have a legal right to harass and torment. But you are free indeed and free in deed! Allow the Holy Spirit to identify the issue, humbly acknowledge your need for grace and forgiveness, disagree with what the enemy says about you and the situation, evict any demonic or ungodly presence, exalt the Lord God, and declare the truth.

Our actions will show that we belong to the truth, so we will be confident when we stand before God. Even if we feel guilty, God is greater than our feelings, and he knows everything (1 John 3:19-20, NLT).

Prayer

Father, I thank You for the gift of emotions. I ask You to help me improve the way I respond to emotion-provoking situations so that the enemy has no foothold in my life. I choose to do the work knowing that You always provide the grace I need. In the name of Jesus Christ, I pray. Amen.

Dealing With Pain

Pain is distracting. Coping with it, whether it is physical or emotional pain, can be exhausting. Because the enemy does not play fair, he will take advantage of us in our pain and vulnerability. His ancient strategy is to attack the weak and weary, the isolated and vulnerable (Deuteronomy 25:17-18). He loves to convince us that our pain is because God does not really love us or care about us. When we believe that lie (often without even realizing it), we will behave out of self-sufficiency, thinking it is up to us to take care of ourselves and protect ourselves from further pain. Thus, we learn to cope with pain independently of God, and that is exactly what the enemy is after because it opens the door to his mischief and malevolence. With God pushed out of the picture, the enemy can torment us with lies about ourselves and others, get us to ruminate, and tempt us into destructive coping mechanisms such as escaping into fantasy, food, drugs, etc. We need a rescue!

Our independent, self-sufficient responses to pain—especially emotional pain—can get so entrenched in our nervous system that we have difficulty even recognizing them as problematic. For example, we may be so used to ruminating and replaying hurtful scenes in our heads, imagining how we wished we had responded differently, that we don't see that such thoughts only serve to keep us in pain. We may welcome judgmental or revengeful thoughts, wishing pain on the one who hurt us, not thinking about the fact that such thoughts serve only to torment us and have no effect whatsoever on the other person. We need to learn to take charge of ungodly thoughts and discard them. If we don't, we inevitably come into agreement with the accuser. And as we've learned, whenever we agree with the enemy and believe the lie that God is not good to us, then we give the enemy the legal right to keep us in a cycle of pain.

Cycle of Pain

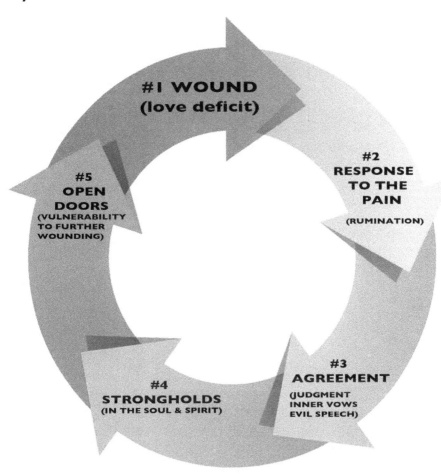

It can be difficult to recognize our need for new God-centered ways of coping, especially if we prefer not to even acknowledge that we are in pain. But freedom from emotional pain and torment starts by being willing to identify and face the pain honestly without blaming God. When we face it and invite God into our pain rather than isolating ourselves and trying to avoid it, He can begin to comfort us, heal us, and show us the next step. Doing so takes effort. It takes a willingness to let our self-protective walls down and admit we need help. It is an act of our will to turn pain-filled rumination into honest, God-centered meditation. But if we have settled it in our hearts that God is good and that He is for us and not against us, then we will want to turn toward Him when we're hurting, not away from Him.

PRACTICAL APPLICATION

If you are in pain right now, for whatever reason, we encourage you to admit it and feel it. Your pain is real, and it is not a sin to feel it. As we have discussed, emotions are information, and they are temporary. It is what we do about our feelings that can be right or wrong. So, if you are feeling some sort of way, openly and honestly invite God into what you're feeling. Allow the truth of his word to guide your actions and bring comfort and peace to your soul. Confess your need for rescue and comfort. The Lord will meet you where you need Him.

Come to me, all you who are weary and burdened, and I will give you rest (Matthew 11:28).

The LORD your God is among you; He is mighty to save. He will rejoice over you with gladness; He will quiet you with His love; He will rejoice over you with singing (Zephaniah 3:17).

Rest in God alone, O my soul, for my hope comes from Him. He alone is my rock and my salvation; He is my fortress; I will not be shaken. My salvation and my honor rest on God, my strong rock; my refuge is in God. Trust in Him at all times, O people; pour out your hearts before Him. God is our refuge (Psalm 62:5-8).

And hope does not disappoint us, because God has poured out His love into our hearts through the Holy Spirit, whom He has given us (Romans 5:5).

... for this reason I bow my knees before the Father, from whom every family in heaven and on earth derives its name. I ask that out of the riches of His glory He may strengthen you with power through His Spirit in your inner being, so that Christ may dwell in your hearts through faith. Then you, being rooted and grounded in love, will have power, together with all the saints, to comprehend the length and width and height and depth of the love of Christ, and to know this love that surpasses knowledge, that you may be filled with all the fullness of God (Ephesians 3:14-19).

Bless the LORD, O my soul, and forget not all his benefits, who forgives all your iniquity, who heals all your diseases, who redeems your life from the pit, who

145

crowns you with steadfast love and mercy, who satisfies you with good so that your youth is renewed like the eagle's. The LORD works righteousness and justice for all who are oppressed (Psalm 103:2-6, ESV).

Disagree: How do I take thoughts captive?

The weapons of our warfare are not physical [weapons of flesh and blood]. Our weapons are divinely powerful for the destruction of fortresses. We are destroying sophisticated arguments and every exalted and proud thing that sets itself up against the [true] knowledge of God, and we are taking every thought and purpose captive to the obedience of Christ (2 Corinthians 10:4-5, AMP).

As a new Christian I (Sally) was told that I needed to "take every thought captive," but I had no idea what that meant. No one explained how! But I tried. If I had a thought that was fearful, judgmental, or ungodly, I would try hard not to think it. But this strategy never really worked. I just ended up feeling like a failure and a terrible Christian. Are "good Christians" just supposed to know how to stop unwanted thoughts, taking them "captive" somehow?

No.

Let's take a moment to do a two-minute thought experiment. When I say "begin," I want you not to think about a panda bear. Do not picture in your mind a fuzzy panda sitting in tall grass munching on eucalyptus leaves. If you start to think about those adorable, fuzzy bears, just stop! Take that thought captive. For two minutes, completely banish panda bear thoughts from your mind. Begin!

How'd that go?

If you're like most of us, it didn't go well at all. Trying to stop a specific thought is not only hard, but also counterproductive. It has the ironic effect of making us more likely to think it.[29] Like holding a bobber underwater, the thought will pop up to the surface when you let go. No wonder my strategy as a new Christian left me feeling like a failure.

It is incredibly important for us to "take our thoughts captive," and it can

---

29 Wegner, D. M. (1994). Ironic processes of mental control. *Psychological Review, 101*(1), 34-52.

be done without ironic pop-up effects. But how? For me, the breakthrough came when I grabbed hold of the entirety of 2 Corinthians 10:5, quoted at the beginning of this section. We are in a spiritual battle. The enemy's plan is mind control—to plant arguments in our thoughts that exalt themselves against the knowledge of God. In other words, the battlefield is our mind. The enemy attacks our thoughts and tries to shoot holes in our faith. He sows seeds of doubt that can grow to become double-mindedness (James 1:6-8). He wants us to doubt God's goodness, love, promises, and purpose for our lives. The thoughts planted by the enemy are designed to exalt themselves above God, to take God's place, to push Him out, to steal our time or our peace, and to leave us drained of faith. We must learn to identify and disagree with every lie of the enemy!

The key to victory is to remember, as we've discussed, that thoughts come from three sources: God, our own mind, or the enemy. The key to taking thoughts captive is being intentional and determined to slow down and examine a thought carefully before agreeing with it or giving it any more time in our heads. This strategy is different from simply pushing a thought down. It takes a bit more work upfront. If a bad thought crosses my mind but is not a thought I want, it isn't my thought. I throw it out immediately! If the thought is an argument trying to "prove" God is not trustworthy, trying to cause doubt, or urging me to be fearful, I know it to be an enemy seed looking for a place to land and grow. I refuse to keep it or let it take root. I then ask Father to help me to shift my thoughts to line up with His.

It is not enough to examine each thought and just throw out the bad ones. We must fill our minds with healthy, Godly thoughts. Whatever our thoughts dwell on will have consequences, either good or bad. You can count on there being fruit to your thought life one way or another. Thoughts, like seeds, grow. It can be stinky rotten fruit or the fruit of the Spirit. Either way, it starts with what we think about, rehearse, agree with, and meditate on. To meditate means to mutter or speak, to roll over and over, to engage in thought or contemplation, to reflect. When we meditate on God's word it produces revelation and understanding.[30]

Revelation means something revealed or disclosed—especially a striking disclosure, as of something not before realized. Revelation comes with an intensity that inscribes truth onto our hearts and minds! Thus, God's revelation brings motivation. Motivation then produces action which

---

30 We are not talking about transcendental meditation, which involves emptying one's mind. Rather, we are talking about Biblical meditation, which involves being filled with scripture and God's thoughts.

147

produces fruit/results. As I learned to take thoughts captive and discard thoughts that were not mine or God's, I would ask the Holy Spirit to help me replace them with His thoughts—with what is true, pure, and lovely. I would think on God's word! I got tired of bad "fruit" like depression, anxiety, and pain—the results of my thinking left to run amuck. I saw in God's word that I did not have to stay stuck in my pain, doubt, and unbelief! Nor do you!

Stuck in a Rut?

At the moment of salvation, our spirits were born again. We have a new nature in Christ. The old is gone and the new has come (2 Corinthians 5:17). Nevertheless, we must work out our salvation (Philippians 2:12). The journey toward mental and emotional freedom is a process. We get stuck in ruts sometimes because we have ruts to get stuck in!

I (Sally) battled with rejection so early in life and for so long that rejection responses (mental and emotional) became my default. After I became a Christian, I received prayer, and that helped me get a measure of victory. But I still did not feel completely free. I prayed about it, and the Lord showed me that the prayer I received had removed the spirit of rejection. With the spiritual component of the stronghold gone, I could begin to see more clearly the mindsets and habit patterns that had developed because of it. As I continued to walk out my spiritual freedom from rejection, the Lord began to speak to me about "soul patterns"—things in my mind, will, and emotions that had worked together with the spirit of rejection to create a powerful stronghold. With the spirit gone, I now had to choose, as an act of my will, to bring my mind and heart into alignment with the spiritual truth that I am free from soul bondage to rejection.

One day my husband and I were driving through the mountains in Colorado. As we headed home it began to rain. It quickly turned into a heavy downpour. As we rounded a corner on the mountain pass, I looked up to see water flowing down the side of the mountain, cascading through deep ruts that had developed over years of rainstorms which had resulted in erosion. As I saw this, the Holy Spirit began to show me the "ruts" I had in my thinking. Just as water takes the "path of least resistance," so does our mind. I had years of ruts—deep, painful ruts—in my thinking. As soon as "rain" (triggers) began, the water filled those ruts before I even knew what was happening. My reactions were automatic, even subconscious. Childhood wounds and the hurts of life had created ruts of brokenness.

I asked the Lord to show me the "ruts" in my thinking and what to do about them. He showed me that I had to be conscious of the process. When one of life's storms started and the "rain" began, such as someone saying something that I perceived as rejection, before allowing the old reactions to take over I had to stop. I had to step out of the rut and take the thought captive before going headlong into old thinking patterns that would lead to major depression. Instead, I learned to ask the Holy Spirit to help me become aware and to slow down my thinking. I needed the Holy Spirit to help me identify the things that triggered my rejection response. Once I began to see those triggers, I would pray for help to stop myself from reacting in old, destructive patterns.

I didn't change overnight; it was a process. But I didn't go it alone, either. Recall the story of Lazarus and Jesus' command to others to unbind him.[31] We need each other. We need to help each other get free. For many of us, interdependence is a hard pill to swallow. We want to be independent and self-sufficient. But that is often a reaction to old pain. We may not want to need others, but we do! There are times we must get over our fear and our pride (yup, I said pride) and ask for help. This was one of those times for me. When I am struggling with rejection, the last thing I want to do is ask for help and risk further rejection! But in those moments, we must decide how badly we want to be free, even when it means doing something hard.

For me, the ruts of rejection and the soul patterns that went with it were so deep that I perceived almost everything as rejection. Because of this I went to a friend who for many years had always told me the truth no matter what—my husband. He is an incredibly loving man, but there is no coddling gene in him! When a situation would happen, I would pray and ask the Holy Spirit to help me to process it and see more clearly from His per-spective. If I was still struggling and/or if the Holy Spirit directed, I would go to my husband and have him pray with me about the situation. The Holy Spirit's wisdom would flow through him, and it was as if in the spirit I could feel him unwinding another layer of those grave clothes off me. Allowing a trusted believer to assist in your freedom is beautiful. Having the privilege of helping in another's freedom as you have been freed is priceless.

A huge part of the freedom I received also came from applying the principle of the "washing of the water of the word" (Ephesians 5:26). If my mind and emotions were telling me I was rejected, I would ask myself, "What does the word say?" I studied who God says I am and chose to believe the word over what my mind and emotions were screaming. The Holy Spirit helped

---

31 See Module 3 on forgiveness.

149

me to fight like Jesus. In Luke 4 Jesus defeated satan with the word of God. If it's good enough for Jesus, it is good enough for us! Though my mind and emotions had learned to perceive rejection and accept it, by my will I chose to believe that God loves me and will never reject me, leave me, nor forsake me (Deuteronomy 31:6, Joshua 1:5, Hebrews 13:5). I am accepted in the Beloved (Ephesians 1:6). I am His pearl of great price (Matthew 13:46).

There were times that the battle got so intense that doing all the above did not seem to bring complete freedom. At those times, I prayed for God to show me if there was more at play. I sought out believers who understood deliverance and would pray about what was at work so that I could receive another layer of freedom. I had to choose to disagree with the enemy's lies and believe the truth of God's word. When I took one step in that direction, the flood that came did not flow into the old ruts of rejection. Rather, the flood became His love washing over me, and it drew me into deeper waters with Him. Meditating over His word brought intense revelation of His amazing love. Of course, I still don't like rejection—no one does. But I know that the One who matters most, the Lover of my soul, loves me with an everlasting love.

PRACTICAL APPLICATION

Learning to disagree with the enemy, to take thoughts captive, and to meditate on the truth takes time and consistent effort. It is easy to get distracted, to let our minds wander, and to leave our thought life undisciplined. But as you may recall, true freedom is the result of commitment, discipline, and fixed habits. Happily, the more we practice meditation the easier it becomes. The more time we spend thinking on what is true, lovely, praiseworthy, and life-giving, the easier it is to discard ugly, unwanted thoughts that run counter to the kingdom of God.

If you are new to Christian meditation, we suggest you start with easy goals and build up endurance. For example, take one scripture and ponder it for just two minutes. When that begins to feel like it's not long enough, increase the time to five minutes. You can build up from there and/or you can work on consistency. If all you have is five minutes of pondering scripture every morning, do that. It will pay off. Freedom comes through commitment and fixed habits!

The following scriptures are helpful for meditating on as we learn to disagree with enemy thoughts and embrace God's truth in our minds and hearts:

Finally, believers, whatever is true, whatever is honorable and worthy of respect, whatever is right and confirmed by God's word, whatever is pure and wholesome, whatever is lovely and brings peace, whatever is admirable and of good repute; if there is any excellence, if there is anything worthy of praise, think continually on these things [center your mind on them, and implant them in your heart] (Philippians 4:8, AMP).

Blessed [fortunate, prosperous, and favored by God] is the man who does not walk in the counsel of the wicked [following their advice and example], Nor stand in the path of sinners, Nor sit [down to rest] in the seat of scoffers (ridiculers). But his delight is in the law of the LORD, And on His law [His precepts and teachings] he [habitually] meditates day and night. And he will be like a tree firmly planted [and fed] by streams of water, Which yields its fruit in its season; Its leaf does not wither; And in whatever he does, he prospers [and comes to maturity] (Psalm 1:1-3, AMP).

Evict: How can I throw out negativity?

It's easy to be negative. In some ways, it's even expected and culturally accepted. Negativity may be directed at ourselves in the form of negative self-talk (self-deprecation), at others in the form of criticism, or at circumstances in the form of complaining. In all its forms, negativity is a toxic attitude that hinders spiritual growth and freedom because it focuses on what is bad or wrong rather than on what is hopeful and helpful. It creates just the sort of dark, dank space the enemy likes to live in. He will keep trying to get us to agree with his ugly thoughts so that he can torment us from the shadows. We must work to eliminate negativity from our speech and enforce its eviction with quick repentance. We don't have to be perfect, but we also don't want to consciously partner with any thought, word, or deed that is negative or unloving.

Easier said than done, we realize. So, in this section we offer practical tips and suggestions that can help you get free of persistent negativity. We focus our teaching on self-deprecation because it is the most accepted form of negativity amongst Christians. We know it is wrong to criticize and complain, but putting ourselves down is not often recognized as a sin or seen as toxic.

Self-deprecation typically comes disguised as humility or humor. It can be

151

obvious or subtle. For example, we may say something like, "I'm such a jerk" or "I'm pretty slow on the uptake." These are obvious putdowns disguised as humility. Or we may say something humorous like, "She's such a kind person. I must have jumped the line when God was giving out compassion." Self-deprecation can be spoken out loud or just heard in our heads. We can do it alone or when someone else is around. Whatever the case, when we engage in self-slander, it hurts the heart of the Father who created us wonderfully well (Psalm 139:14).

When I (Julie) studied the term self-deprecation, what I learned was life changing. First, the root of "deprecation" is the English word "precatory," from the Latin *precari* which means to pray or to express an earnest request or plea. Second, the Latin prefix *de* means "to remove from, to reverse, or to make the opposite of." When you put *de* and precatory together, you get "deprecation," which means to remove or ward off by prayer. When you deprecate yourself, then, you are literally praying against yourself and removing blessing by your own earnest request or plea. Self-deprecation is like praying, "Father, please don't bless me or see any value in me." When we consistently devalue and belittle ourselves through self-deprecation, we are cursing ourselves and wishing away the blessing of love, grace, and mercy—the values we all deeply crave and need. Self-deprecation hurts the heart of God. He loves us utterly and longs to bless us. He desires that we see ourselves as He sees us: worthy, valued, and dearly loved.

For many of us who grew up with unresolved trauma and unmet needs, self-deprecation has become a habit that we hardly know we have. And it can be hard to break. Truth is easier to understand than to apply. It's not usually enough to say, "Oh, now I realize I shouldn't put myself down, so I won't do it again." But the message of this module is that we can be free in deed, and it is our responsibility to put what we know into action. The key is to develop the discipline and commitment that results in new habits. We must work to get what we know in our heads to drop into our spirits so that it affects our choices.

PRACTICAL APPLICATION

If you know that self-deprecation is a habit of yours, then this practical application is for you. If you are not sure, pray about it or ask a close friend. You might not be aware of how often you put yourself down, but a friend is likely to be. If you don't struggle with self-deprecation, per se, you may have other negative verbal or mental habits, such as complaining or criticizing. Toxic negativity in all its forms needs to be evicted. These exercises can help.

To begin, ask the Lord to forgive you for any way in which you have partnered with negativity. Receive His forgiveness. Then evict any spirit of self-deprecation, complaining, or criticism. Without legal right, it must go. There is no condemnation in Christ, and He wants to help you walk in freedom! As a follow-up, consider doing one or more of these exercises:

1. **Trash the negativity.** Research shows that when you write down a thought and then physically throw it away, it will have less influence on your attitudes than if you do not throw it away.[32] In other words, literally trashing a negative thought lessens its impact. It's not necessarily an instant fix, but over time it can help. You've got nothing to lose by trying it except the negative thoughts you don't want anyway.

Begin by writing down any negative thoughts you have about yourself (or others) and the hurtful things people (or you) have said. Such utterances are word-curses, and the intent of this exercise is to expose and dispose of them. We suggest you use a separate piece of paper for each label, lie, or recurring negative thought. Use scrap paper if you want, but a whole piece of paper will feel more significant than a scrap. You might end up with a bunch of thoughts. Here are some examples:

I'm ugly.   I'm stupid.
I'm not worth listening to.   I'm unlovable.
I'm hopeless.   I'm helpless.
I'll never amount to much.   I'm such a jerk.

---

32 Brinol, P., Gaso, M., Petty, R. E., & Horcajo, J. (2013). Treating thoughts as material objects can increase or decrease their impact on evaluation. *Psychological Science,* 24(1), 41-47.

I'm weird	I'm _____.
I'm such a loser.	I hate _____.
No one will ever find me desirable.	

After you have written out each thought, crush each piece of paper, each individual word-curse against yourself or others. Now slam-dunk it into the nearest trash bin. We're serious! Get up out of your seat and chuck it like you mean it, declaring "I renounce this negative, lying thought in the name of Jesus Christ!"

If a thought you trashed (or a new one) comes to mind persistently, repeat the exercise as necessary and without putting yourself down for having to work at it!

2. Declare a fast! While preparing for a week-long fast with a ministry team, I (Sally) asked the Father what kind of fast He wanted me to do. Rather than what I expected, I heard Him tell me to fast self-deprecation. Although the Holy Spirit has done much work in my heart and mind to cast out self-rejection and self-ridicule, this fast served as a refresher course, reminding me not to let those thoughts lurk in the shadows. For the week, I asked the Father to help me examine my thoughts. If something self-deprecating came to mind, I would immediately throw the thought out. As I consistently disagreed with the enemy and discarded his ugly thoughts without owning them or beating myself up for them, I began to see myself more in line with how the Father sees me. Getting rid of those negative thoughts made more room for hearing God's thoughts!

If you struggle with rejection or shame, it is likely that self-deprecation came along as a package deal. To put the word into action, try a self-deprecation fast—a time set aside to intentionally slow down your thoughts so that you can avoid negative self-talk. Allow the Holy Spirit to identify any thoughts that do not line up with His thinking about you. Meditate on how He sees you.

Sometimes rejection and/or shame lead us to blame-shift and see everything that is wrong in others rather than ourselves. In this case, self-deprecation may not be your struggle. Instead, you may find yourself chronically finding fault with others. The suggestion of a fast is still a good one. In this case, you may frame it as a fast from negativity, criticism, judgment, or complaining. You might be amazed at how many negative thoughts you have in a day, whether they are directed at yourself, others, or circumstances. Setting aside this time to declare a fast and seek the Father's heart can help reveal the need to have your mind renewed and begin a new level of sanctification in your thinking. It can also help to reveal strongholds that may need further deliverance.

3. Hold on to the truth. The research study about trashing thoughts reported another important finding. If you write down a thought, fold the paper, and put it in your pocket for safekeeping, the thought has a greater impact on your subsequent attitudes than thoughts you don't value enough to put in your pocket. So, consider writing down what God says about you in His word. The Bible has a lot to say about how God sees you. You can use the following suggestions or pray and read scripture for yourself to hear what God says to you personally.

I'm wonderfully made (Psalm 139:14).
I'm valuable and loved (Isaiah 43:4).
I'm accepted (Ephesians 1:6, KJV).
I'm forgiven (Ephesians 1:7).
I can do all things through Christ who gives me strength (Philippians 4:13).
I am free indeed (John 8:36).
I am safe (Proverbs 18:10, 29:25; 2 Timothy 4:18).
I am a new creation in Christ (2 Corinthians 5:17).
I am God's workmanship, and all He does is good (Ephesians 2:10).

Now fold that piece of paper and put it in your pocket. At the end of the day, put it in your Bible for safekeeping. Treat it as a valuable reminder of the truth. As often as needed, pull it out and declare the truth out loud!

Whether you try one, two, or all three of these suggestions, we strongly recommend that you tell a trusted friend that you are committed to overcoming negativity. We have held one another accountable in this process, and we still catch one another periodically. We want to agree with what the Lord says about us, and sometimes we need the reminder to listen to the right voice! If you are faithful to these exercises, your thoughts and feelings about yourself (and others) will become less and less negative and more and more consistent with the truth that you (and they) are loved, valuable, accepted, wonderfully made, strong in the Lord, and free indeed!

Exalt: Who and what am I looking at?

In the 1990s, neuroscientists discovered mirror neurons, a type of neuron in the brain that fires both when doing something (like grasping a bottle) and when observing an action (as when someone else grasps a bottle).[33] Mirror neurons help explain why when a mother smiles at her infant, the infant smiles

33 https://www.nature.com/articles/d43978-021-00101-x

back and why we tend to match the posture, facial expressions, and gestures of the person we're talking to.[34] Because the same neurons are involved in both observing and doing, observing an action (such as watching someone crack an egg into a pan) can help us learn to do the same thing.

The existence of mirror neurons is consistent with what scripture teaches: We become like the one we behold. If we mirror the posture and facial expressions of the people with whom we interact, how much more should we mirror the posture and attitude of Jesus. We need to spend time with Him and observe His ways. We need to exalt the Lord and fix our eyes on Jesus, the author and finisher of our faith (Hebrews 12:2). To exalt comes from Latin root words that mean upward/outward (ex) and high (altus). So, to exalt means to look up and see the greatness and glory of God. The more we gaze upon His glory and goodness, the more our lives will mirror His goodness. When we look at Jesus and really see Him—the way He loved the Father, the way He loved people, the way He spoke and acted and felt and prayed—the more we become like Him.

Have you ever thought about the idea that we are drawn to light because God is light (1 John 1:5)? The truth is humans crave light. We can stare at it for hours! A friend of ours, a veteran minister to India and the Himalayas, has observed this phenomenon among the goat herders of isolated mountain ranges. In this age of satellite internet, she has seen these rural mountain men staring into their cell phones watching television or scrolling social media instead of watching their goats! We stare into our "light boxes" as she calls them (cellphones, iPads, tablets, televisions, laptops) because we crave light. Or is it that we really crave the God who is light? Most of us long for a deeper understanding of our identity and purpose. Do we think that watching other people fall in love, solve problems, have adventures, and cope with their everyday lives will help us figure these things out for ourselves? Do we hope that viewing someone else's trials and triumphs will make our own lives easier to bear? Are we learning anything by spending so much time with these substitutes rather than looking to the One who made us and gives us purpose (Ephesians 2:10)?

Only God can truly show us who we are and how to live. I (Julie) grew up with powdered milk, imitation vanilla, and television for a friend. I survived, but I can tell you, each of these is inferior compared to the real thing. As you continue your journey into greater freedom, we encourage you to set some boundaries around the time you spend on your lightboxes. Crave the real thing! Know that what you spend time gazing at and looking up to will be what you tend to mimic. Jesus understood the importance

---

34 https://www.verywellmind.com/what-is-the-chameleon-effect-5114522

of guarding what His eyes beheld, and He declared with confidence and humility that He could do nothing on His own but only did what He saw His Father doing (John 5:19-20). Take encouragement from His example! Let's exalt the Lord, gazing often and long at His glory and goodness!

The eye is the lamp of the body. If your eyes are good, your whole body will be full of light (Matthew 6:22).

Truly, truly, I tell you, whoever believes in Me will also do the works that I am doing. He will do even greater things than these, because I am going to the Father (John 14:12).

One thing I have asked of the LORD; this is what I desire: to dwell in the house of the LORD all the days of my life, to gaze on the beauty of the LORD and seek Him in His temple (Psalm 27:4).

PRACTICAL APPLICATION

If you own a device that gives you a weekly screentime report, consider setting a goal to steadily decrease screentime each week until it is at a level that you can feel good about. You may want to pray about it and ask the Lord to help you set realistic goals. At the same time, you may also want to set a goal to spend more time reading your Bible or a good book, listening to worship music or praying, spending time outside in the beauty of nature or inside at an art museum, or any other positive activity that keeps the eyes of your heart open to beauty and love of God. To walk free INDEED involves consistently choosing to fix our eyes on Him, exalting Him above all else.

Declare: To whom and what am I committed?

Even as we endeavor to keep our eyes fixed on Jesus, we can take encouragement in knowing that He is looking in our direction, too! He is actively looking for those He can strongly support. By definition, a support holds something up, bears most of the weight, keeps something upright, or gives assistance. We need all that strong support as we walk out our freedom in Christ! Who, then, does the Lord strongly support? Those whose hearts are blamelessly inclined toward Him (not literally blameless or perfect). He supports those who declare their commitment to walking in obedience.

For the eyes of the LORD run to and fro throughout the whole earth, to give strong support to those whose heart is blameless toward him (2 Chronicles 16:9a, ESV).

These words were spoken to Asa, king of Judah. Asa was a good king. Early in his reign, he faced an army of a million Cushites and their 300 chariots. Asa had half that many men and no chariots. In his desperation, he cried out to the Lord for help, and the Lord gave him a great victory. He routed the enemy and profited from the plunder (2 Chronicles 14). Asa did what was right in the eyes of the Lord and there was peace for many years. In 2 Chronicles 15, we read how Asa brought the people back into covenant relationship with the Lord. He removed idols, cleaned up the temple, repaired the altar, and led the people to renew their commitment to love and serve Yahweh only. He even removed his own mother from her position as queen mother because she worshipped Asherah. Asa had a heart that was "wholly true" (*shalem im*) all his days (2 Chronicles 15:17 and 1 Kings 15:14).

This phrase "wholly true" (*shalem im*) is similar but not identical to the one translated as "blameless toward" (*shalem elaw*) in 2 Chronicles 16:9. In both, the word *shalem* can mean blameless, wholly true, fully devoted, perfect, complete, peaceful, cherishing friendship.[35] The important difference is the preposition *elaw* (toward) versus *im* (with). According to scripture, Asa cherished friendship with the Lord all his days—even when his actions suggested otherwise. I don't know about you, but there have been significant moments in my life when I (Julie) have had a clear choice to follow the Lord or turn away. My heart has been *shalem im*, and I have stayed with the Lord even when my head did not fully understand what was happening and even when my emotions didn't enjoy the circumstances.

But, like Asa, I haven't always acted like I was fully devoted to the Lord, moving toward Him. You see, the first part of the verse that we like to quote from 2 Chronicles 16:9 is part of a rebuke given to Asa after he messed up. Late in his reign, he got irritated with Baasha, the king of Israel. Rather than seeking the Lord for guidance as he'd done when he faced the Cushites, Asa took care of Baasha himself, out of his own resources. He paid the King of Syria using much of the wealth and plunder he'd gotten years earlier after routing the Cushites. Asa's act of self-sufficiency and self-reliance—after all

---

35 www.biblehub.com

those years of peace and devotion to the Lord—hurt the Father's heart. So, He sent a prophet, Hanani, to speak to Asa. Here's the whole speech:

Because you relied on the king of Syria, and did not rely on the Lord your God, the army of the king of Syria has escaped you. Were not the Ethiopians [Cushites] and the Libyans a huge army with very many chariots and horsemen? Yet because you relied on the Lord, he gave them into your hand. For the eyes of the Lord run to and fro throughout the whole earth, to give strong support to those whose heart is blameless toward him. You have done foolishly in this, for from now on you will have wars (2 Chronicles 16:7b-9, ESV).

The same man whose heart was fully devoted/blameless with the Lord (*shalem im*) all his days had a moment when his heart did not move blamelessly toward the Lord (*shalem elaw*). The Lord was grieved to be robbed of the chance to strongly support Asa. The Lord is constantly looking out for the one whose heart is moving toward His heart out of loving allegiance—a loyal commitment to obedience. He doesn't require our blameless perfection. But He is looking for our inclination to move toward Him rather than away from Him. When He finds such a heart, God runs to fully support that person (Luke 15:20).

So, what does all this mean for us? To be truly and practically free, we need to keep moving toward the one who loves us completely just as we are. He will support our efforts to choose Him. Every time we choose obedience, we experience increased freedom to make the next right choice! To be practically free doesn't mean to be perfect, but it does mean that we are moving toward Him and receiving more and more of His loving support.

Note that the rest of Asa's story is a sad cautionary tale. Even though his heart remained with the Lord all his days, this failure to move toward the Lord became a failure that Asa allowed to defeat him at the end of his life. He reacted with pride and shame when he messed up, and he could not bring himself to repent of his self-reliance. He chose to suffer through disease rather than face up to his sin. Maybe he felt he deserved it. Maybe a punishing spirit tormented him. Whatever the case, his life didn't end on a note of victory, freedom, or peace. He chose a "bird's eye" view and took his pain out on others:

Asa was angry with the seer and became so enraged over this matter that he put the man in prison. And at the same time Asa oppressed some of the people. Now the rest of the acts of Asa, from beginning to end, are indeed written in the Book of the Kings of Judah and Israel. In the thirty-ninth year of his reign, Asa became diseased in his feet, and his malady became increasingly severe. Yet even in his illness, he did not seek the LORD, but only the physicians. So in the forty-first year of his reign, Asa died and rested with his fathers (2 Chronicles 16:10-13).

In our journey toward greater freedom in Christ, let's keep reminding each other that it is a heart that moves toward God that catches His eye. Let us be quick to repent and open to receiving mercy (Romans 2:4). No matter how much we grow and no matter how much we falter, God is looking to strongly support us when we who move toward Him and know we need Him (Matthew 5:3). Whatever is in your storehouse, the treasures, resources, abilities, or talents you hold, they are the Lord's. He doesn't bless us with large victories so we can forget Him during the little ones. He longs for heart-to-heart connection. He doesn't expect perfection. Therefore, we don't need to be afraid to admit our weaknesses, mistakes, or failings. We need simply to keep moving toward God, walking out the practicalities of our freedom in Christ with Him.

Declaration of Allegiance

Lord, right here and right now, I declare and pledge my heart's allegiance to You and You alone. I choose to keep moving toward You, Lord, in faithful obedience. I thank You that Your loving eyes look on me with tenderness and compassion. I thank you for your loyal love and full support as I walk this freedom road. Thank you, Father, that Your enduring love never fails or fades. You do not judge or feel disappointment at my missteps. Thank You for Your faithfulness, daily mercy, and endless grace. Amen.

Can I learn from my mistakes?

Yes!

From an early age, I (Julie) developed the idea that to avoid shame and the pain of being laughed at, I had to get things right. Mistakes were not okay. My desire to look smart often trumped my desire to learn. The irony is that this approach typically leads to less learning because the focus is on the appearance of mastery rather than actual mastery. According to researcher Carol Dweck, people with a mindset like this see mistakes, effort, and slow progress as a sign of hopeless inability. Therefore, they tend to avoid hard things and give up quickly in the face of obstacles.[36]

In truth, mastery develops through effort and persistence despite mistakes,

36 https://www.mindsetworks.com/science/Impact

obstacles, or setbacks. Mistakes are an integral part of the learning process. Feedback is useful, not threatening, because it helps us course correct. In over 30 years of research, Dweck has observed that individuals who pursue actual mastery (a "growth mindset") over the appearance of mastery (a "fixed mindset") end up achieving more in life and developing a greater sense of freedom. Being stuck in a fixed mindset leads to a narrowing of life experiences, less joy, and a reduced sense of freedom.[37]

I still don't like to make mistakes. No one does. But I have chosen to embrace the fact that mistakes are opportunities to grow up rather than reasons to give up. It's pointless to try to appear accomplished, righteous, or perfect before the Lord. He knows better! He knows my weak frame and is mindful that I am dust (Psalm 103:14). I have nothing to prove. I remind myself of the kind intentions of His will (Ephesians 1:5) and the fact that His correction is always for my good (Romans 8:28, Hebrew 12:7). I have nothing to fear from Him because He is perfect love (1 John 4:8, 18). Can I learn from my mistakes? Yes! Mistakes aren't obstacles, they are opportunities!

To illustrate, I made a very instructive mistake a few years ago while shopping with my 14-year-old son. I learned a lot that day about my own lingering insecurities, and it was an opportunity to grow up just a little bit more. It was a simple interaction, but it helped me see just how fragile my sense of autonomy and personal control was at the time and how my fear of being controlled and manipulated hurt the people I love.

The weather was hot that day, and we had already been to three stores. On route to our last store, my son told me he was thirsty. We were near a fast-food place, so I figured I'd drive through and get him something. But I didn't tell him that. Instead, I teased him by saying I was thirsty too as I drank the last few sips of water out of my insulated cup!

"That's mean," he said. "When I'm shopping with GG, she always gets me a drink." This interaction wasn't particularly unusual. Good-natured teasing is how we roll sometimes. I could have continued in that light-hearted vein and carried on toward the drive-through. Instead, I reacted negatively. I felt manipulated. I started to respond with annoyance in my tone, but he interrupted to say, "I know. If I hadn't said anything you would have gotten me a drink."

He was right. I had intended to get him a drink. But after his comment, my reaction was to lock in on my control as the mom and not allow him to manipulate me. He didn't get his drink. I skipped the drive through, made our

---

37 *Ibid.*

last quick stop, and headed home in silence.

In that silence, the Lord began to reveal the irony of what had just happened. In trying to preserve my sense of control, I had given it away. I had allowed my son's words to influence my actions. I had already decided to stop and get him a drink. So why didn't I just do that? Because of an allergic reaction to the idea of being manipulated. Ironically, I ended up getting manipulated in the spiritual realm. I did not respond in love. Instead, I had partnered with self-protection and let it influence my decision to deny my son a drink. We both got robbed.

Honestly, as embarrassing as this incident may be, I am grateful for the lesson. It helped me learn to identify enemy influence more quickly so that I can freely choose how to respond. Love would have been more concerned about the thirst of a 14-year-old boy than about maintaining its own rights (1 Corinthians 13:5). Instead, I responded in the soul realm out of a self-centered need for control. Fear of being controlled may not be your "allergy." Maybe you are allergic to rejection or shame or pain. Whatever it is, if the Lord has revealed it, He wants to help you walk free in action and deed. The more we are settled in our identity as free from the tyranny of the evil one, the better equipped we are to battle old habit patterns. Our part is to ask the Holy Spirit to help us quickly identify enemy interference and be willing to obey what He says to do. We must also be quick to repent, willing to learn from our slip-ups, and willing to keep putting in the effort to walk in freedom.

Prayer

Lord, please help me to learn from my mistakes. Settle my identity in you. I want to respond to others from a place of freedom and love. Identify for me when the enemy is trying to influence my thoughts and actions, and help me to disagree with it quickly. I want to respond with Your love—the perfect love that drives out fear and shines a bright light on spirits of darkness. When I mess up, Lord, let Your kindness lead me to repent quickly (Romans 2:4). You are faithful, and You have promised to strengthen me and guard me from the evil one (2 Thessalonians 3:3). You alone can keep me from stumbling (Jude 1:24). I need you! I love you! Amen.

Do I have to contend for my freedom?

Yes.

It's not necessarily easy to establish a "new normal." Freedom can feel unfamiliar and even uncomfortable. Uncertainty over what it's like to live free of our usual anger, fear, expectation of rejection, shame, or whatever can tempt us to choose what is familiar over what is freedom. We can easily take the path of least resistance and allow ourselves to slip back into familiar soul patterns rather than fight for new ones. But if we are willing to put in the work, committed to moving toward the Father's heart, He gives us the grace we need to walk in that newness. Our work is to believe (John 6:29)! The freedom we have in Christ is real. When we ask the Holy Spirit to help us, He will. He will alert us to temptation and give us grace to effectively resist giving in to old patterns.

The more we intentionally and prayerfully practice new ways of thinking, feeling, and behaving, the more our efforts will pay off. All of it matters and works together. The more we practice thinking in a manner consistent with the word of God and our new freedom, the easier it will be to feel free and act free. Likewise, if we choose to act free regardless of how we feel, then that choice will make it easier for our thoughts and feelings to follow suit. Because we are spirit, soul (mind, will, emotions), and body, all these facets are connected. God will help work it all together for our good and for His glory! (Romans 8:28)

PRACTICAL APPLICATION

In contending for my freedom, it has helped me (Sally) tremendously to think of old thought patterns as an old address I no longer live at. He helped me move out and move on. When my thinking would try to return to old destructive patterns, the Holy Spirit would remind me that I don't live there anymore. We encourage you to ask the Holy Spirit to remind you of this truth when you need it most. If a trigger tries to drag you back into a rut or start you driving down a familiar road to nowhere good, stop and remember that it's a place you don't live at anymore! You no longer have the keys to that house. It isn't your furniture. It's no longer comfortable! It's not for you. We pray that this will help you put the brakes on old habits so that you can hear the Holy Spirit's directions and reset your GPS!

Free INDEED: A Final Review

As we've tried to explain and exemplify, the process of walking out our freedom involves six steps, made easy to remember by the acronym INDEED. To *identify* the issue, ask the Father to reveal any areas in which He wants you to seek healing and freedom. Next, acknowledge that you *need* Jesus and the wisdom of the Holy Spirit in all things (Proverbs 3:5, John 14:26). Our freedom is in Christ alone. Draw near in humility (James 4:8) because He is the way, the truth, and the life (John 14:6). The path to freedom is through the power of the cross. Wholeheartedly *disagree* with any lies or ungodly beliefs that the Lord reveals to you and ask the Holy Spirit to "unpack" any ways in which you have believed the lie that God is not good. Be single-minded in your determination to disagree with any lie that insults the love and goodness of God! Then, having dealt with any legal issues in the spirit (like forgiveness and repentance), boldly *evict* (cast out) any tormenting or evil spirit that is coming against your freedom or still trying to speak lies to your soul. Now look up! *Exalt* the Lord for His goodness. Give Him thanks and praise for His great love and faithfulness. He loves to hear your voice (Song of Solomon 2:14)! Finally, *declare* the truth that sets you free (John 8:32) and stay committed to walking out your freedom.

This Book of the Law must not depart from your mouth; meditate on it day and night, so that you may be careful to do everything written in it. For then you will prosper and succeed in all you do (Joshua 1:8).

I am the LORD your God, who brought you out of the land of Egypt so that you would no longer be slaves to the Egyptians. I broke the bars of your yoke and enabled you to walk in uprightness (Leviticus 26:13).

I run in the path of your commandments, for you have set my heart free (Psalm 119:32, NHE).

And I will walk in freedom, for I have sought Your precepts (Psalm 119:45).

We encourage you to keep studying the word and being intentional in your journey toward becoming free indeed. To that end, we leave you with scriptures for further study and two powerful declarations to use, a Declaration of Freedom and a Declaration of Dependence.

Scriptures for Further Study

I - Identify the Issue

John 8:31-32 (You will know the truth and the truth will set you free)
John 16:13 (When the Spirit of truth comes, He will guide you into all truth)
Luke 11:9-10 (Ask, seek, knock—He will respond)
Philippians 1:9-11 (May your love abound with all knowledge and depth of insight)
Ephesians 1:17 (Pray that the Father gives you spirit of wisdom and revelation)
1 Corinthians 4:5 (He will bring to light what is hidden in darkness)

N - Need Jesus

Ephesians 2:8 (By grace you have been saved...)
John 14:6 (I am the way, the truth, and the life)
Romans 3:23 (All have sinned and fall short of the glory of God)
1 John 1:9 (If we confess our sins, He is faithful and just)
Hebrews 12: 10-11 (He disciplines us for our good)
Revelation 12:11 (They conquered him by the blood of the lamb)
Titus 3:4-7 (He saved us, not because of works done by us in righteousness)

D - Disagree

John 8:44 (Satan is a liar and the father of lies)
Revelation 12:10 (The accuser of the brothers has been thrown down)
Romans 8:1-2 (Therefore, there is now no condemnation)
Titus 3:3 (We were once foolish, disobedient, deceived/led astray)
Matthew 12:30 (He who is not with Me is against Me)
1 John 4:1-6 (Test the spirits)

E - Evict

Luke 9:1 (He gave them power and authority to cast out demons)
Matthew 10:8 (Heal the sick, raise the dead...cast out demons)
Matthew 16:19 (Whatever you bind on earth is bound in heaven)
1 John 4:4 (He who is in you is greater than He who is in the world)
Acts 8:7 (Unclean spirits came out of many)
Acts 16:18 ("In the name of Jesus Christ I command you to come out")
Mark 16:17 (In My name they will drive out demons)

E - Exalt the Lord

Psalm 35:27 (Exalted be the Lord who delights in His servant's well-being)
Jude 1:24-25 (Now to Him who is able to keep you from stumbling... glory!)
Daniel 4:37 (I praise and exalt and glorify the King of heaven)
Psalm 99:5 (Exalt the Lord our God and worship at His footstool)
Song of Solomon 2:14 (Let Me hear your voice)
Psalm 147:1 (How pleasant and lovely it is to praise Him)
Psalm 118:14-16 (The Lord is my strength and my song)
Psalm 21:13 (Be exalted, O Lord; we will sing and praise Your power)

D - Declare the Truth (see also the Declaration of Freedom)

Romans 6:22 (Now that you have been set free from sin...)
Romans 8:37-39 (In all these things we are more than conquerors)
2 Thessalonians 3:3 (He will strengthen you and protect you from the evil one)
Galatians 5:1 (For freedom Christ has set us free; stand firm therefore)
2 Peter 1:3 (His power has given us all we need for life and godliness)
Psalm 107:17-22 (Declare His works with rejoicing)
Psalm 35:28 (My tongue will proclaim Your righteousness)

Declaration of Freedom

I know and declare the truth that sets me free indeed[38]

I was chosen by Love before the foundation of the world. I am a child of the King. I have been adopted in love through Jesus Christ.[39] I declare my faith in Jesus and the finished work of the cross. I declare that I am truly, legally, and practically free. Jesus set me free so that I could truly walk in freedom. I honor Him now by choosing to stand firm in that freedom and by refusing to submit again to the slavery of sin and iniquity.[40] I declare that in Christ Jesus I am legally free from condemnation and legally free from the law of sin and death.[41] I declare that my life is now hidden with Christ in God,[42] hidden in the light of God. I choose to walk in the light as He is in the light,[43] and I give permission to the Holy Spirit to bring to light any hidden thing that keeps me from walking in my freedom.[44] As He does, I will confess and renounce sin and unrighteousness knowing that He is faithful to forgive and cleanse me completely.[45] I have been crucified with Christ and buried with Him in baptism, so now I am also raised with Him. I am seated with Christ in the heavenlies and blessed with every spiritual blessing.[46] I declare that I am in Christ and therefore I am a new creation—a fresh, unprecedented piece of handiwork created by Christ to do good things![47] I receive His strength in my inner being, having my spirit, mind, will, and emotions rooted and grounded in the love of God. By faith I want to know this love that goes beyond knowing. I want to be filled with all the fullness of God.[48] I exalt you, Lord, for You delight in my well-being, my healing, and my freedom in spirit, soul, and body.[49] I give You thanks and declare Your good work in my life with rejoicing.[50]

---

38 John 8:31-32
39 Ephesians 1:4-5
40 John 8:36; Galatians 5:1
41 Romans 8:1-2; Colossians 2:13-15
42 Colossians 3:3
43 1 John 1:7
44 1 Corinthians 4:5
45 1 John 1:9
46 Galatians 2:20; Colossians 2:12, Ephesians 1:3 and 2:6
47 2 Corinthians 5:17; Ephesians 2:10
48 Ephesians 3:16-19
49 Psalm 35:27; 1 Thessalonians 5:23; 3 John 2
50 Psalm 107:22

Declaration of Dependence

When in the course of human events it becomes necessary for God's people to dissolve the spiritual bands which have connected them with other false and tyrannical gods and to assume the separate and peculiar station to which the Laws of God invite them, a decent respect to their own weakness of will requires that they should declare the causes which impel them to the separation.

We hold these truths to be evident, having been revealed by the Spirit of God, that humankind is created in the image of God and endowed by Him with one certain and unalienable right: free will, the right to choose. We thereby choose to exercise our freedom. We choose to reject spiritual tyranny. We choose to become sons and daughters of Liberty. We pledge our allegiance to God's Way, His Truth, and His Life. We choose Christ, the embodiment of all that makes for temporal and eternal life, liberty, and happiness. It is the right of God's people to alter and abolish all ties with the enemy of our souls, satan, and to institute a new government on earth as it is in heaven. The kingdom of heaven, alone, provides the principles and powers by which we may experience eternal safety and happiness. It is evident to all who have eyes to see and ears to hear that satan has governed humankind with disastrous results since the fall. His insufferable evils, his long train of abuses and usurpations, cause us now by our right and duty, to throw off his governance and to no longer agree with or be subject to his torment. The history of this king of darkness is a history of repeated injuries and usurpations, all having in direct object the establishment of an absolute tyranny over humankind.

To prove this, let facts be submitted to a candid (sincere, honest, open-minded) world:

His purposes are to kill, to steal, to destroy, to take the fullness of life from God's people.

> The thief comes only to steal and kill and destroy. I have come that they may have life, and have it in all its fullness *(John 10:10).*

He has defiled the minds of God's children.

> [Inasmuch as we] refute arguments *and* theories *and* reasonings and every proud *and* lofty thing that sets itself up against the [true] knowledge of God; and we lead every thought *and*

purpose away captive into the obedience of Christ (the Messiah, the Anointed One) *(2 Corinthians 10:5, AMPC).*

He has endeavored to destroy and devour.

> Be well balanced (temperate, sober of mind), be vigilant *and* cautious at all times; for that enemy of yours, the devil, roams around like a lion roaring [in fierce hunger], seeking someone to seize upon *and* devour *(1 Peter 5:8, AMP).*

He deceives people into believing his time is not short.

> Therefore be glad (exult), O heavens and you that dwell in them! But woe to you, O earth and sea, for the devil has come down to you in fierce anger (fury), because he knows that he has [only] a short time [left] *(Revelation 12:12, AMPC).*

He exerts power over humankind even though he is defeated.

> *And* having spoiled principalities and powers, he made a show of them openly, triumphing over them in it *(Colossians 2:15, KJV).*

He has intimidated and bullied humans to believe he holds power he does not have unless it is given to him through agreement.

> Behold! I have given you authority *and* power to trample upon serpents and scorpions, and [physical and mental strength and ability] over all the power that the enemy [possesses]; and nothing shall in any way harm you *(Luke 10:19, AMPC).*

He cannot speak truth.

> You belong to your father, the devil, and you want to carry out his desires. He was a murderer from the beginning, refusing to uphold the truth, because there is no truth in him. When he lies, he speaks his native language, because he is a liar and the father of lies *(John 8:44).*

There is no justice, no peace, no life without Jesus. The enemy has plundered, ravaged, and destroyed the lives of God's people. He works to complete his works of death, desolation, and tyranny.

We solemnly publish and declare that we are free from the devil's tyranny, absolved from all allegiance to him. All connection between us ought to be and is totally dissolved through Jesus Christ. We are completely free children of God. And for the support of this Declaration, with a firm reliance on the protection of divine Providence, we pledge to King Jesus ALONE our life, our fortune, and our sacred honor. We resist the devil and his governing over us. We sever agreement with him and fully submit to the Lordship of Christ Jesus.

> Submit yourselves, then, to God. Resist the devil, and he will flee from you *(James 4:7)*.
>
> And they answered, Believe in the Lord Jesus *Christ* [give yourself up to Him, take yourself out of your own keeping and entrust yourself into His keeping] and you will be saved, [and this applies both to] you and your household as well *(Acts 16:31, AMP)*.
>
> The God of peace will soon crush Satan under your feet. The grace of our Lord Jesus Christ be with you *(Romans 16:20)*.

Sally Randall   *Julie Jacks*

FOR FURTHER READING

Apologetics

Lewis, C. S. (1960). *Mere Christianity.* Macmillan.

McDowell, J. (1979). *Evidence That Demands a Verdict.* Here's Life Publishers.

McDowell, J. & Stewart, D. (1980). *Answers to Tough Questions Skeptics Ask About the Christian Faith.* Tyndale House.

McDowell, J. (1990). *A Ready Defense.* Here's Life Publishers.

Strobel, L. (1998). *The Case for Christ: A Journalist's Personal Investigation of the Evidence for Jesus.* Zondervan.

Healing and Deliverance

Anderson, N. T. (1990). *The Bondage Breaker.* Harvest House Publishers.

Anderson, N. T. (1990). *Victory Over the Darkness: Realizing the Power of Your Identity in Christ.* Regal Books.

Anderson, N. T. (2001). *The Steps to Freedom in Christ.* Bethany House.

Clark, R. (2015). *The Biblical Guidebook to Deliverance.* Charisma House.

Hammond, F., & Hammond, I. M. (1990). *Pigs in the Parlor*. Impact Christian Books.

Hammond, F. (1991). *Demons and Deliverance in the Ministry of Jesus*. Impact Christian Books.

Heiser, M. S. (2020). *Demons: What the Bible Really Says about the Powers of Darkness*. Lexham Press.

Hogue, R. (2008). *Forgiveness*. Rodney Hogue.

Horrobin, P. (2003). *Healing Through Deliverance, Volume 1: The Foundation of Deliverance Ministry*. Chosen Books.

Horrobin, P. (2003). *Healing Through Deliverance, Volume 2: The Practice of Deliverance Ministry*. Chosen Books.

Kylstra, C., & Kylstra, B. (2005). *Biblical Healing and Deliverance: A Guide to Experiencing Freedom from Sins of the Past, Destructive Beliefs, Emotional and Spiritual Pain, Curses and Oppression*. Chosen Books.

Lewis, C. S. (1961). *The Screwtape Letters*. Macmillan.

Lozano, N. (2010). *Unbound*. Chosen Books.

Moore, B. (2000). *Breaking Free*. Billy Graham Evangelistic Association.

Pagani, A. (2018). *The Secrets to Deliverance: Defeat the Toughest Cases of Demonic Bondage*. Charisma House.

Prince, D. (1998). *They Shall Expel Demons*. Chosen Books.

Savard, L. (1993). *Shattering Your Strongholds*. Bridge-Logos Publishers.

Wright, H. (2009). *A More Excellent Way*. Whitaker House.